CAN SINGAPORE FALL?
MAKING THE FUTURE FOR SINGAPORE

IPS-NATHAN LECTURES

CAN SINGAPORE FALL?
MAKING THE FUTURE FOR SINGAPORE

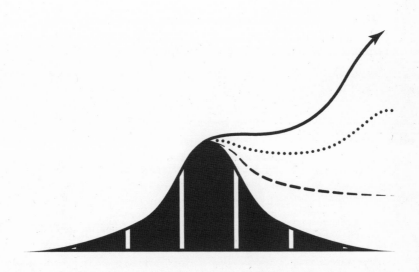

LIM SIONG GUAN

Published by

World Scientific Publishing Co. Pte. Ltd.
5 Toh Tuck Link, Singapore 596224
USA office: 27 Warren Street, Suite 401-402, Hackensack, NJ 07601
UK office: 57 Shelton Street, Covent Garden, London WC2H 9HE

British Library Cataloguing-in-Publication Data
A catalogue record for this book is available from the British Library.

CAN SINGAPORE FALL?
Making the Future for Singapore

ISBN 978-981-3238-07-7
ISBN 978-981-3238-62-6 (pbk)

For any available supplementary material, please visit
http://www.worldscientific.com/worldscibooks/10.1142/10935#t=suppl

Desk Editor: Sandhya Venkatesh

Typeset by Stallion Press
Email: enquiries@stallionpress.com

Printed in Singapore

THE S R NATHAN FELLOWSHIP FOR THE STUDY OF SINGAPORE

AND THE IPS-NATHAN LECTURE SERIES

The S R Nathan Fellowship for the Study of Singapore was established by the Institute of Policy Studies (IPS) in 2013 to support research on public policy and governance issues. With the generous contributions of individual and corporate donors, and a matching government grant, IPS raised around S$5.9 million to endow the Fellowship.

Each S R Nathan Fellow, appointed under the Fellowship, delivers a series of IPS-Nathan Lectures during his or her term. These public lectures aim to promote public understanding and discourse on issues of critical national interest.

The Fellowship is named after Singapore's sixth and longest-serving President, the late S R Nathan, in recognition of his lifetime of service to Singapore.

Other books in the IPS-Nathan Lecture series:

The Ocean in a Drop — Singapore: The Next Fifty Years
by Ho Kwon Ping

Dealing with an Ambiguous World
by Bilahari Kausikan

The Challenges of Governance in a Complex World
by Peter Ho

CONTENTS

FOREWORD

This series of three lectures on the theme "Can Singapore Fall?" was composed out of a concern for the survivability and sustainability of Singapore.

That Singapore has survived and succeeded for just over 50 years is no guarantee of its survival and success in the next 50 years, or beyond. And, in fact, we must know that just continuing on the path of yesterday is to guarantee a future that will not be so bright, possibly even a future that may not be there.

I do not mean to be dramatic or melodramatic here. But having spent 37 years in the Singapore Civil Service, with five years as Head of the Civil Service, and having had the privilege of observing how Mr Lee Kuan Yew and Dr Goh Keng Swee, the pre-eminent leaders among Singapore's founding fathers, thought and acted, I felt it necessary to share my views as to how to better assure a good future for the generations to come. This was why I accepted the S R Nathan Fellowship.

While the theme of the lecture series is "Can Singapore Fall?", one will soon realise that the real question I wanted to pose is, "*Will* Singapore Fall?" — except that, if I were to set it as such, it might sound a little pre-deterministic and pessimistic. So, "Can Singapore Fall?" is a more neutral question. Obviously, however, when we ask the question in that way, the answer can only be, "Of course, it can." The real challenge is to find a way to think and act, so as to minimise the likelihood of Singapore falling.

Where the future is too difficult to predict, a "strategy" of reacting to events or simply doing what is agreeable and popular will be both foolhardy and irresponsible. Where the future is unclear and unpredictable, it becomes absolutely critical to start with a vision of where we want to get to or what we want to become, and then think through what we need to do to get there. It is in thinking of what we need to do that we weigh the realism of our vision and adjust our plans accordingly.

The essential starting question is, "What kind of Singapore do we want in the next 10, 20, 50, 100 years? What is the Singapore we would like to see (if we were still alive then) when SG100 (100 years of Singapore's independence, the year 2065) comes around?" We could take the attitude that SG100 will happen anyway — just be patient and wait. But this could then simply be a case where, "to wait and see is to wait and die."

SG100 will be the time of the fourth generation of Singaporeans since independence in 1965. For many Singaporeans today, this will not be the generation of our children or even grandchildren. It is the generation of our great grandchildren.

One may find it ludicrous to think of Singapore in 50 years when no one can even be clear what the future would be like in 10 years. But if we think that way, then we are thinking in a reactive mode, where we need to know a situation before we can think of what to do. Instead, we should be thinking of a future we can shape and create, even though we may be a small country, subject to events and developments in the world that are often beyond our control.

No doubt, each generation of Singaporeans must solve its problems in its own way. However, some problems take several decades to take root, and some matters take consistent effort over a generation to prevent them from becoming intractable problems. These are the issues that require courage and wisdom today, so that future generations will not curse the current generation for a profound dereliction of duty.

My first lecture described Singapore as "The Accidental Nation", a nation unplanned in its creation and unexpected in its survival. But while there is much that can be learnt from the past, it would not be adequate for the future. My second lecture was on "The Fourth Generation" of Singaporeans since independence. This is the generation whose days will include SG100. And my third and final lecture was on "The Way of Hope", which dicussed how we can best secure a future for the generations to come.

I believe that Singapore had managed to survive and progress since independence because we paid a lot of attention to honour. We honour our word, always, by being trustworthy and dependable; we honour one another, always, by appreciating and respecting one another, keeping the peace, and being united. We made Singapore something out of "nothing" by building a strong "nation brand".

The Honour Circle starts with honour-driven individuals, who will do all they can with their talents and abilities. This builds up honour-driven families, where children grow in self-confidence and strong values, which they imitate from and practise with their parents and siblings. We then go to honour-driven communities, of which a Gracious Society is a key feature. Next, we have honour-driven organisations, which may be businesses or civic organisations, where superior leadership allows people to be the best they can be and do the best they can in pursuit of innovation, excellence and outwardness. Finally, we have the honour-driven nation, where culture and values and clear leadership in government and our national institutions create the foundation for honour-driven individuals to thrive and be the best they can be.

We have reached the status of a First-World Economy. What is the First-World Society we wish to be? What would be right for Singapore and Singaporeans, not just for the current generation but for the generations to come? In the end, it is the kind of society we want to be and the sustainability of such a society that are the crucial issues.

I look ahead with optimism. I believe we can look forward to a thriving, successful Singapore if we:

- Maintain our nation brand value of integrity and trustworthiness
- Use our diversity in race, language, culture and religion for synergistic effect
- Have facility with technology and continuous change

- Focus on identifying, developing and harnessing talents and abilities at all levels
- Release the energy and imagination of the young to be involved in national life
- Take advantage of the rise of Asia, the Internet and the middle class
- Urgently establish a culture of innovation, excellence and outwardness

What I set out in my lectures is my vision of what we need to be in both social and economic terms, based on my conviction that what I propose is both practical and practicable. But there can be neither finality nor perfection in these ideas. If every young Singaporean, whether in school or university or just starting out in life, would spend time to study and debate the lectures, it would lend clarity and hope for their future and that of their descendants.

ABOUT THE MODERATORS

Tan Tai Yong is the President and Professor of Humanities (History) at Yale-NUS College. He has been a faculty member of the Department of History at the National University of Singapore (NUS) since 1992. Professor Tan is also Honorary Chairman of the National Museum of Singapore.

Kuik Shiao-yin is a Nominated Member of Parliament in the 12th and 13th Parliament of Singapore (2016-Present). She is the Co-Founder and Director of The Thought Collective, a group of social businesses in Singapore that aim to build up the social and emotional capital of the city.

Gillian Koh is Deputy Director (Research) at the Institute of Policy Studies, where she leads research in the areas of party and electoral politics, civil society, state-society relations, and citizen engagement in Singapore. She obtained her PhD in Sociological Studies from the University of Sheffield.

Lecture I
THE ACCIDENTAL NATION

This lecture series is based on the theme, "Can Singapore Fall?", but you will realise in the course of my speech that the real question that I want to ask is, "*Will* Singapore Fall?" — except that, if I were to set it as such, it might sound a little pre-deterministic and a little too pessimistic for everyone. So, "Can Singapore Fall?" is a more neutral question, but obviously, when you ask a question like that, the answer must be, "Of course it can, if you make the conditions as bad as you can possibly imagine." Let us get to it, and hopefully along the way, we can learn from one another, and gather ideas from one another on how we can act in a way to minimise the possibility or likelihood of Singapore falling.

The Melian Dialogue

The Peloponnesian War was a war fought between Athens, leading the Peloponnesian League, and Sparta, leading the Delian League. It stretched from 431 to 404 B.C., and included what has come to be known as the famous Siege of Melos.

Melos is an island in the Aegean Sea more than 100 kilometres to the east of mainland Greece. It was a prosperous island. The Melians were of the same ethnic group as the Spartans, but they chose to remain neutral in the war. Athens invaded Melos and asked Melos to pay tribute to Athens. The Melians had never paid tribute to Athens before, and refused to do so now.

Thucydides, the Athenian historian, wrote about what has come to be known as the Melian Dialogue. It describes the negotiations between Athens and Melos. The Athenians' approach was to appeal to the Melians' sense of pragmatism, pointing to the Athenian army's overwhelming strength and their "reasonable" terms for surrender. The Melians, on the other hand, appealed to the Athenians' "sense of decency". Whether or not Melos was truly neutral, ships could freely resupply there; this made Melos strategically important for Athens and subduing Melos would reduce the reach of Sparta's navy.

In substance, the Melian Dialogue went as follows:

ATHENS
Surrender and pay tribute to Athens, or
be destroyed.

Refusing to argue with the Melians on questions of morality, the Athenians simply assert, **"The strong do what they have the power to do and the weak accept what they have to accept."**

MELOS
We are a neutral city, not an enemy. There
is no need to conquer us in your war with
Sparta.

ATHENS
If we accept your neutrality and independence, we would look weak. Our people
would think that we have left you alone
because we are not strong enough to conquer you.

MELOS

If you invade us, it will alarm the other neutral Greek states, who will then turn against you lest the same fate befalls them.

ATHENS

The Greek states on the mainland are unlikely to act this way.

MELOS

It would be shameful and cowardly for us to submit without a fight.

ATHENS

It is only shameful if there is a reasonable chance of defeating the attacker. There is no shame to submit to a superior opponent.

MELOS

Although you are much stronger, we would regret not trying to fight as there could still be a chance to win.

ATHENS

This is a foolish hope. It does not come from rational analysis and is just an emotional response.

MELOS

The gods will help us because our position is morally just.

ATHENS

The gods will not intervene. It is natural that the strong dominate the weak.

MELOS

Sparta will help defend us.

ATHENS

The Spartans are a practical people. They will not put themselves at risk when their interests are not at stake. Besides, we have the stronger navy. There is no shame in submitting to a stronger enemy offering reasonable terms. **What makes sense is to submit to superiors, stand firm against equals, and be moderate to inferiors.**[1]

The Melians stuck to their position. Athens mounted a siege and finally captured the city in 416 B.C., executing the men, and enslaving the women and children. Some modern historians look at it as an act of genocide, a wiping off the face of the earth of an entire nation, culture, and civilisation.

The Melian Dialogue is often quoted as a classic case study in political realism, where power is assumed to be the primary goal of political acts.

Don't Be Weak

I asked a foreign friend whether the Melian Dialogue carried a lesson for Singapore. His response was immediate and direct. "The lesson for Singapore is straightforward. **Don't be weak.** Don't be weak in how you are perceived externally by others. Don't be weak internally."

---

[1] Adapted from *The Melian Dialogue* (416 B.C., Thucydides, V.84-116). University of Warwick. https://warwick.ac.uk/fac/arts/classics/students/modules/intohist/usefuldocuments/thucydides_V.84-116.pdf.

I start my series of IPS-Nathan Lectures with this reference to the Melian Dialogue because "Don't be weak" explains so much of Singapore. The continuous existential question for Singapore is how to respond to the argument that **"What makes sense is to submit to superiors, stand firm against equals, and be moderate to inferiors"**, and especially on how Singapore can live under the observation that **"The strong do what they have the power to do and the weak accept what they have to accept."**

Singapore's quest for survival and self-determination has been with us from at least 1959, when Singapore attained internal self-government. Our struggle for independence and sovereignty will continue for all our years ahead.

Singapore, to my mind, is **"The Accidental Nation"**, a nation unplanned in its creation and unexpected in its survival. My lecture today will survey how we came to be, and how we should think of the future. How does "Don't be weak" explain our past, and how must "Don't be weak" make our future?

My next lecture will be on **"The Fourth Generation"** of Singaporeans since independence. It is the generation whose days will include SG100. And my third and final lecture will be on **"The Way of Hope"**, discussing my beliefs on how we can best secure a future for our generations to come.

The "Accident" of Independence

The founding political leadership of Singapore led by Mr Lee Kuan Yew had not believed that Singapore *could* be on its own or *should* be on its own. This was the real world that the rational pragmatist could not escape from.

Singapore was a British colony and had been part of the Straits Settlements comprising Penang, Melaka and Singapore. Singapore was geographically part of the Malay Peninsula, keeping it separate from the Federation of Malaya was to go against the facts of geography and history, even from the days before Sir Stamford Raffles founded modern Singapore in 1819.

Yet, the British had carved Singapore out of Malaya while integrating Penang and Melaka into the Federation of Malaya because Singapore hosted the largest British military establishment east of Suez. Singapore was critical for the sustenance of the British Empire.

Thus, the British granted the Federation of Malaya independence on 31 August 1957, while only granting Singapore full internal self-government in 1959, where the colonial administration controlled external relations and security, including internal security.

The People's Action Party led by Mr Lee Kuan Yew had, as a prime feature of its election manifesto for the General Elections that brought it to power in 1959, the aim of seeking to be reunited with Malaya. The principle of "Don't be weak" drove Singapore to find strength in the bigger political entity. Malaya did not welcome the idea of merger with Singapore. Singapore's predominantly Chinese population would have tilted the overall racial balance in an unwelcome way.

> The continuous existential question for Singapore is how to respond to the argument that "What makes sense is to submit to superiors, stand firm against equals, and be moderate to inferiors", and especially on how Singapore can live under the observation that "The strong do what they have the power to do and the weak accept what they have to accept."

That Malayan politics was very much built upon ethnic lines did not make merger with Singapore an attractive proposition. On the other hand, the possibility of Singapore turning communist under the tutelage of Mao's China was a most unpleasant prospect. A communist Singapore at the southern tip of the Malay Peninsula would have perhaps been a worse nightmare to the Malayans than a communist Cuba would have been to the Americans.

In 1963, the Prime Minister of Malaya, Tunku Abdul Rahman, was persuaded that he had to consider the idea of merger as something that would be good for Malaya. The prospect of Kuala Lumpur being the Washington, D.C. of the merged entity, the political centre, with Singapore as the New York, the commercial centre, had its attractiveness. The challenge of ethnic distribution was ameliorated by including Sabah and Sarawak in the merger while offering the British a way out for granting independence not just to Singapore, but also its Borneo colonies.

I can clearly recall the strains of songs, which spoke of the hopes of being in Malaysia, in particular:

> Let's get together,
> Sing a happy song,
> Malaysia forever,
> Ten million strong.

Land of the free,
Marching as one.
Ready to share in every way,
So let's get it done — get it done, get
it done.

We're all in the same boat,
Steady as you go.
Let's pull together,
Everybody row — row, row, row.

It's right, it's the answer,
There's no other way,
To be good neighbours everyday

Malaysia forever, evermore,
United for liberty,
Home of the happy people,
Just you wait and see — wait and
see, wait and see, wait and see.

Let's get together,
Sing a happy song,
Malaysia forever,
Ten million strong.

We're ready for merger,
Let's open the door,
To Malaysia forever,
Ever more![2]

---

[2]Bobby Gimby, *Malaysia For Ever* [Recorded by Marymount Vocational School, 1963]. Accessed 29 November 2017. https://www.youtube.com/watch?v=PtEBs98AFOY.

You get the idea — it is quite a nice song. The logic of merger with Malaya was so intuitive that few questioned it. Even fewer in Singapore believed that Singapore could go it alone as an independent and sovereign nation.

"Don't be weak" drove us to merger in 1963; "Don't be weak" turned us towards independence in 1965.

Thus, Malaysia Day, 16 September 1963, came with much hope and happiness, like long-lost siblings brought back together to make the family complete again. But the family reunion was not to last. Two racial riots in Singapore, in July and September 1964, brought to the fore racial distrust between the Malays and the Chinese.

In the economic sphere, Singapore sensed that the economic benefits to be expected from the merger of equal partners might not be forthcoming. Signals from Kuala Lumpur portended a weakening of Singapore, both economically and politically. As the political differences grew more acrimonious over the months, both Kuala Lumpur and Singapore came to the conclusion that the best way forward would be for Singapore to leave Malaysia.

Singapore became an independent sovereign state on 9 August 1965. What had been deemed by Mr Lee Kuan Yew and his economic czar, Dr Goh Keng Swee, to be an impractical way forward for Singapore, became the only practical way forward. Thus was born The Accidental Nation: not planned for nor hoped for, but the best of bad options. **"Don't be weak" drove us to merger in 1963; "Don't be weak" turned us towards independence in 1965.**

Singapore, the Little Red Dot

If you look at an atlas of the world, Singapore, the country, fits quite nicely in the letter "O" in its name. I do not know whether any of you have ever thought about it that way. If you look at this map behind me, there is a big red circle.

That is not Singapore. Singapore is the dot in the centre of the circle, and even then, the dot is bigger than what Singapore is, geographically, for that map. Singapore fits in the letter "O" in the name of the country. Maybe that is something most of us do not quite realise until it is mentioned. Indeed,

Mr Lim Siong Guan speaking at the first lecture of his IPS-Nathan Lectures series.

in most atlases, they have to make a point of skewing the scale by enlarging the dot that represents Singapore so that it may be pointed out. That is how small Singapore is. The question is, how do you keep the country sovereign and independent despite its smallness?

What are the implications for survival, security, and success for a small state like Singapore? Singapore had to find its own way while facing racial tensions internally and unfriendly forces externally, with little by way of an army to defend herself. Singapore was extremely vulnerable. Malay ultranationalists in Malaysia were denouncing Singapore, and Indonesia was still conducting *Konfrontasi* (military confrontation) against Singapore because

Indonesia had deemed the formation of Malaysia in the merger of the Federation of Malaya, Sabah, Sarawak, and Singapore in 1963 a neo-colonialist plot.

When President B. J. Habibie of Indonesia referred to Singapore as a "little red dot" in 1998, he might have meant it as a disparaging remark. Little would he have expected that Singaporeans would take it up as a badge of honour, a symbol of succeeding despite the odds. Singapore had reached out beyond its immediate surroundings and "leapfrogged" the region to adopt the whole world as its hinterland, its source of capital, investment, research and technology, management capability, and, most of all, markets — there is no point working on industrialisation and having all the factories if you produce stuff that cannot be sold anywhere. Singapore is the result of human imagination and endeavour.

In less than two generations, Singapore had attained First-World status economically and had become a guide and a hope for other developing countries. From 1965 to 2015, Singapore's per capita Gross Domestic Product at Current Market Prices increased over a hundred fold, from US$516 to US$53,630. What factors enabled Singapore to succeed?

The Legacy of Lee Kuan Yew

In 2015, Singapore commemorated its 50th year of independence with much celebration and stirring pride. It was also a year marked by national mourning, with the demise of its founding prime minister, Mr Lee Kuan Yew, on 23 March 2015.

In the days following Mr Lee's passing, there were many comments on his legacy — quite a few equated Singapore's physical transformation into a modern metropolis and imaginative developments, such as the Marina Barrage, with Mr Lee's legacy.

However, this would be a superficial way to think of Mr Lee's legacy. The material accomplishments of Singapore are but evidence that what Mr Lee and the founding generation of leaders dared to do was right. The real legacy of Mr Lee Kuan Yew is the indomitable spirit that drove him and our founding fathers to do all that they could to secure the survival and well-being of the nation and its people. "Don't be weak" as a crucial principle for national survival and success never escaped Mr Lee's heart and mind. And he was fully vindicated by Singapore's peace, progress and prosperity in the years since independence.

Singapore's success in its first 50 years is the story of a brand — a nation brand of trustworthiness. We all understand the meaning of brands, whether it is in the way you choose your clothing, the shoes you are going to buy, or where to go for your next vacation. Whatever it is, brands mean something, and if a brand has a high standing, that is the brand you go after (if you can afford it). Nations also have nation brands. Singapore is a story of making success out of nothing, building the nation brand as an antidote to being no more than a "little red dot". No natural resources. No natural markets. A small population. A tough neighbourhood.

Honouring our *word* is one critical aspect of the Singapore brand as a nation. There is a second critical aspect, which also relates to *honour*, but this time about society. It is about Singaporeans honouring one another, appreciating our social differences, our diversity, and at the same time seeking strongly to maintain social harmony as a common good for all.

Singapore has, from its early days, been multi-racial, multi-lingual, multi-cultural and multi-religious. Mr Lee Kuan Yew had recognised from the start that race, language, culture, and religion are visceral issues; they go to the very heart of our individual identities and drive emotions that can easily overwhelm reason. People will kill each other for reasons of race or religion. So much of what we see in the media, day after day, affirm this point. Internal discord will split Singapore asunder. Mr Lee Kuan Yew, in his wisdom, decided from early on that religion, for example, shall be safeguarded as a matter for individual choice, but the rules must be strict so that no one may exercise his right on religion in a way that impedes his neighbour's freedom to similarly exercise his choice of religion.

Honour, the Singapore Brand

In summary, Singapore is a construct built upon two strong legs of honour. The first is the nation brand of trustworthiness, we are a country and a people who *honour our word*. The second is being a nation where diversity of race, language, culture and religion is recognised as a fact of life to be sustained in social harmony by a people who *honour one another*.

Brand Finance, a leading international brand valuation and strategy consultancy firm based in London, identified Singapore as the top nation brand in 2015, in its ranking of nation brands across the world. It found Singapore to be the top nation brand again in 2016 (and, most recently, also 2017), with Hong Kong as Number Two and Switzerland as Number Three, followed by other European countries and New Zealand, with Japan coming at Number 10. The United States was not in the list of top 10 nation brands. Do note, however, we are talking here about the brand strength where Singapore was Number One; when it came to brand value, the United States was Number One.

Brand Finance, in the foreword of its *Nation Brands 2016* report, stated:

> The effect of a country's national image on the brands based there and the economy as a whole is now widely acknowledged. In a global marketplace, it is one of the most important assets of any state, encouraging inward investment, adding value to exports and attracting tourists and skilled migrants. The results of this year's Brand Finance Nation Brands report show the benefits that a strong nation brand can confer, but also the economic damage that can be wrought by global events and poor nation brand management.[3]

In its *Executive Summary of Nation Brand Strength* in 2016, Brand Finance wrote:

> Singapore last year claimed the title of World's strongest Nation Brand and has held off close challenges from Hong Kong and Switzerland to do the same again this year. Nation Brand value is reliant upon GDP (i.e., the revenues associated with the brand). Singapore's small size means it will never be able to challenge for the top spot in brand value terms, because its brand simply cannot be applied extensively enough to generate the same economic uplift

---

[3] Brand Finance, *Nation Brands 2016*, October 2016, http://brandfinance.com/images/upload/nation_brands_2016_report.pdf.

as "brand USA" for example. However, in terms of its underlying nation brand strength, Singapore comes out on top.[4]

As for religious diversity, the Pew Research Center, a non-partisan American think tank based in Washington, D.C., which provides information on social issues, public opinion, and demographic trends shaping the United States and the world, found Singapore in 2014 to be the most religiously diverse country in the world.[5] What is remarkable is how social peace has been maintained and sustained despite this huge diversity.

Singapore has managed to survive and prosper as an independent country since 1965, despite even Mr Lee Kuan Yew himself not believing this was possible when he sought merger with Malaya. It was an achievement founded on fundamental perspectives of building a nation that had nothing by way of natural resources, little by way of land and population, and a diversity of race and religion, which many countries would find an imponderable challenge. But *will* this success last? *Can* this success last?

Can Singapore Fall? Will Singapore Fall?

The Chinese have a saying "富不过三代" (fù bù guò sān dài) or "Wealth does not last beyond three generations". After celebrating its 50th year, Singapore is moving into its third generation. Will Singapore's wealth and stability last?

Sir John Bagot Glubb (1897–1986) was a British soldier, scholar, and author, who led and trained Transjordan's Arab Legion between 1939 and 1956. After his retirement from the British army, he wrote a profound essay, *The Fate of Empires and Search for Survival*, which analyses the lifespan of great nations from their genesis to their decline.[6]

---

[4] Ibid.

[5] Pew Research Center, "Global Religious Diversity", 4 April 2014, http://www.pewforum.org/2014/04/04/global-religious-diversity/.

[6] John Bagot Glubb, *The Fate of Empires and Search for Survival* (Edinburgh: William Blackwood & Sons, 1976).

Glubb notes that, over the last 3,000 years, the "periods of duration of different empires at varied epochs show a remarkable similarity." Glubb explores the facts, and notes that most great nations do not last longer than 250 years (or 10 generations), and many last for much shorter periods of time.

Here is his summary:

The Nation	Dates of rise and fall	Duration in years
Assyria	859–612 B.C.	247
Persia (Cyrus and his descendants)	538–330 B.C.	208
Greece (Alexander and his successors)	331–100 B.C.	231
Roman Republic	260–27 B.C.	233
Roman Empire	27 B.C.–A.D. 180	207
Arab Empire	A.D. 634–880	246
Mameluke Empire	1250–1517	267
Ottoman Empire	1320–1570	250
Spain	1500–1750	250
Romanov Russia	1682–1916	234
Britain	1700–1950	250

Glubb also observes that "immense changes in the technology of transport or in methods of warfare do not seem to affect the life expectation of an empire" — it merely changes the "shape of the empire".

In his essay, Glubb describes many of the stages of empire and many of the reasons why they break down and eventually disappear.

According to Glubb, the stages of the rise and fall of great nations seem to be as follows:

HIGH NOON

Age of Pioneers / Age of Conquests / Age of Commerce / Age of Affluence / Age of Intellect / Age of Decadence / Decline

Let us examine the stages.

Age of PIONEERS

Initiative
Enterprise
Courage
Hardihood

First, the **Age of Pioneers**. A small nation, treated as insignificant by its contemporaries, suddenly emerges and conquers the world. This age is characterised by an extraordinary display of energy and courage.

Pioneers are ready to improvise and experiment: "Untrammelled by traditions, they will turn anything available to their purpose. If one method fails, they try something else. Uninhibited by textbooks or book learning, action is their solution to every problem."

The first stage of life of a great nation is a period of amazing initiative, enterprise, courage, and hardihood. These qualities produce a new and formidable nation.

The second stage of expansion consists of more organised, disciplined, and professional campaigns. Methods employed tend to be practical and experimental.

Let us then consider the **Age of Conquests**.

Age of CONQUESTS

Glory
Honour
Commercial Prosperity

The nation acquires the "sophisticated weapons of old empires" and a great period of expansion ensues. The principal objects of ambition are glory and honour for the nation.

The conquests result in the "acquisition of vast territories under one government", thereby birthing commercial prosperity. Basically, the observation is that, in the Age of Conquests, the young man thinks that the best thing he can do for himself is to be a soldier, to fight for king and country.

So we come to the **Age of Commerce**.

Age of COMMERCE

Courage
Patriotism
Devotion to Duty

The main purpose of this era is to create more wealth. The first half of this age seems to be splendid: "The ancient virtues of courage, patriotism, and devotion to duty are still in evidence." The nation is proud and united, and boys are still required to be manly. In addition, courageous initiative is displayed in the quest for profitable enterprises all around the world.

But the acquisition of wealth soon takes precedence over everything else. The previous objectives of "glory" and "honour" are but "empty words, which add nothing to the bank balance" for the people.

This is the period of time when values start shifting from the self-sacrifice of the pioneers to self-interest.

Thus we come to the **Age of Affluence**.

Age of AFFLUENCE

Materialism
Defensiveness
Excess
Change from service to selfishness
Increase in selfishness, desire for wealth and ease
Weakening sense of duty

Money causes the people to gradually decline in terms of courage and enterprise. Wealth first hurts the nation morally: "Money replaces honour and adventure as the objective of the best young men... the object of the young and ambitious is no longer fame, honour, or service, but cash."

Instead of seeking wealth for their nation or community, men seek wealth for their own personal benefit. The divide between the rich and poor increases, and the wealth of the rich is flaunted for people to see. People enjoy high standards of living, and consume in excess of what they need.

Education is also affected negatively. Instead of seeking learning, virtues, and qualifications that serve the nation, parents and students seek qualifications that enable them to grow rich.

The transition from the Age of Conquests to the Age of Affluence is a period that Glubb calls "High Noon".

While the immense wealth of the nation impresses other nations, this period reveals the same characteristics in each case he studied, namely:

- The change from service to selfishness
- Defensiveness

Describing the change from service to selfishness, Glubb says that during this period, "enough of the ancient virtues of courage, energy, and patriotism survive to enable the state successfully to defend its frontiers. But beneath the surface, greed for money is gradually replacing duty and public service."

As for defensiveness, the rich nation is no longer interested in glory or duty, but is preoccupied with the conservation and maintenance of its wealth and luxury. Money replaces courage and subsidies are used to "buy off" enemies.

History indicates that nations decline not because its people do not have a conscience, but because of:

- A weakening sense of duty
- An increase in selfishness and the desire for wealth and ease

The Age of Affluence describes the pinnacle of the empire. Next comes the **Age of Intellect**.

Age of INTELLECT

Endowing works of art
Patronising music and literature
Founding of endowing institutions of higher education

During this stage, wealth is no longer needed for necessities or luxuries, and there are also abundant funds for the pursuit of knowledge. Businessmen that made their wealth in the age of commerce seek fame and praise of others by:

- Endowing works of art
- Patronising music and literature
- Founding or endowing institutions of higher education

It is ironic that while civilisations make advancements in science, philosophy, the arts, and literature, and the spread of knowledge seems to be one of the most beneficial of human activities, history shows us that every period of the decline is characterised by the expansion of intellectual activity.

Why is this so?

The answer is "NATO" — **No Action, Talk Only.** Intellectualism leads to discussion, debate, and argument, which is often seen around the world today. But this "constant dedication to discussion seems to destroy the power of action."

Intellectualism, selfishness, and the lack of a sense of duty to one's family, community, and nation, all appear simultaneously in the nation.

The most dangerous by-product of this Age of Intellect is the birth and growth of the notion that human intellect can solve all the problems of the world, when in fact the survival of the nation really depends on its citizens.

In particular, in order for that nation to thrive and survive, its citizens must display:

- Loyalty
- Self-sacrifice

So, finally, we come to the **Age of Decadence and Decline.**

Age of DECADENCE

Materialism
Defensiveness
Frivolity
Pessimism
An influx of foreigners
The welfare state
Weakening of religion

Decadence is a mental, moral, and spiritual disease that disempowers its people to the extent that they do not make an effort to save themselves or their nation because they do not think that anything in life is worth saving.

The Age of Decadence comes about due to the following factors:

- Extended period of wealth and power
- Selfishness
- Love of money
- Loss of a sense of duty

It is marked by seven characteristics:

- Defensiveness
- Pessimism
- Materialism
- Frivolity
- An influx of foreigners
- The welfare state
- Weakening of religion

Let us consider each of these characteristics.

Defensiveness: People are so consumed with defending their wealth and possessions that they fail to fulfil their duty to their family, community, and nation. Glubb also notes that another remarkable and unexpected sign of national decline is civil dissension and intensification of internal political hatred. Various political factions hate each other so much that, instead of sacrificing rivalries to save the nation, internal differences are not reconciled, leading to a weaker nation.

Pessimism: As the nation declines in power and wealth, universal pessimism invades its people and accelerates its decline.

Materialism: People enjoy high standards of living, and consume in excess of what they need.

Frivolity: As the pessimism invades its people, people start to think, "Let us eat, drink and be merry, for tomorrow we die." The people forget that material success is the result of courage, endurance, and hard work, and spend an increasing part of their time indulging in sex, leisure, amusement, or sport. The heroes in declining nations are the athlete, the singer, or the actor; not the statesman, the general, or the literary genius.

Influx of Foreigners: In his essay, Glubb observes that one frequent phenomenon in the decline of empires is the influx of foreigners. Foreigners are attracted by affluence and take on jobs that the citizens often do not want to do themselves. But they can be weak links in the society for various reasons. For instance:

- They will be less willing to sacrifice their lives and property for their new nation
- They form communities of their own that protect their own interests above that of their new nation

While the immense wealth and growth of our nation has "dazzled other nations", some Singaporeans have expressed concern over a possibly decreased sense of public duty with a change from service to selfishness; there is a growing defensiveness, and desire to grow and retain individual wealth.

Glubb states that, just by being different, foreigners tend to introduce cracks and divisions in the society. The important point here is that the citizens themselves would have to stand up for the nation, because they cannot leave the defence of the nation to foreigners.

The Welfare State: As history shows, the decline of a nation is often preceded by a tendency towards philanthropy and sympathy.

As Glubb states, "The impression that it will always be automatically rich causes the declining empire to spend lavishly on its own benevolence, until such a time as the economy collapses, the universities are closed, and the hospitals fall into ruin." The welfare state is just another milestone in the life story of an ageing empire in decline.

Weakening of Religion: Glubb defines religion as "the human feeling that there is something, some invisible Power, apart from material objects, which controls human life and the natural world." Religion does not only mean institutionalised faith, but represents a set of moral values that in turn influence social norms. Without morality, men are more likely to snatch than serve, and the spirit of self-sacrifice is weak.

The nation is characterised by defensive-minded militaries, decaying morals, loss of religion, frivolous consumption of food, entertainment and sex, and the complete focus on individual interests.

Where is Singapore?

You may be wondering, at this point: Glubb's essay is about empires; could it apply to a small state like Singapore?

Glubb mentions in his essay that, "If the small country has not shared in the wealth and power, it will not share in the decadence."

Has Singapore shared in the wealth and power? If we accept that Glubb's essay is possibly applicable to Singapore, which age is Singapore in?

Based upon social observations of increased materialism and consumerism, could it be that Singapore has experienced its "High Noon" and is somewhere between the Ages of Affluence and Decadence? While the immense wealth and growth of our nation has "dazzled other nations", some Singaporeans have expressed concern over a possibly decreased sense of public duty with a change from service to selfishness; there is a growing defensiveness, and desire to grow and retain individual wealth.

As Glubb described in his essay, the Age of Affluence is one where "the object of the young and ambitious is no longer fame, honour or service, but cash." Does that describe Singapore in some way?

Singapore also registers certain markers of the Age of Intellect, which is a stage where wealth is no longer needed for necessities or luxuries, and there are also abundant funds for the pursuit of knowledge.

Another sign that Singapore could be thought of having reached the Age of Intellect is the increase in discussions, debates, and arguments, especially on social media, without a focus on action, or leaving the action as something for others to do.

Please do not get me wrong. I am not here to make judgments on what is good or bad about our individual choices; I am only making observations on where Singapore seems to be, and what implications these portend if we think Glubb has a relevance for Singapore.

It is interesting to note that, in the rise of nations to the Age of Affluence, it is the striving for economic wealth that was the prime *motivator*. Whereas in the social decline and decay which followed in the empires, it is affluence that was the prime *enabler*. Thus, **affluence is at the root of both the rise and the fall of the nations,** as one empire gives way to another that is more energetic, more imaginative, and more determined to establish the strength and influence of its nation.

Of the seven characteristics of the Age of Decadence, we could note that there are already signs of at least five of them in Singapore, namely:

1. Defensiveness
2. Pessimism
3. Materialism
4. Frivolity
5. Influx of foreigners

Of the remaining two characteristics of the "welfare state" and the "weakening of religion", we could note that:

Welfare State: In Singapore's early years of nation-building, the emphasis in its social policies was self-reliance. But in recent times, there has been a shift to collective responsibility. While the government has been quick to emphasise that this shift to collective responsibility does not mean self-responsibility is less important, this shift could be a slippery slope if the people and government were to let their guard down, and collective responsibility slowly takes on the face of collective irresponsibility.

I offer you another story from ancient Greece that we can learn from. Ancient Greece was the pioneer of democracy 2,500 years ago. How did democracy in ancient Greece come to an end?

One of the experts on the history of the period was Edith Hamilton (1867–1963). In her book, *The Echo of Greece*,[7] on Athen's decline, she wrote:

> What the people wanted was a government that would provide a comfortable life for them, and with this as the foremost object, ideas of freedom and self-reliance and service to the community were obscured to the point of disappearing....

> Athens was more and more looked on as a co-operative business possessed of great wealth in which all citizens had a right to share. The larger and larger funds demanded made heavier and heavier taxation necessary, but that troubled only the well-to-do, always a minority, and no one gave a thought to the possibility that the source might be taxed out of existence. Politics was now closely connected with money, quite as much as with voting. Indeed, the one meant the other. Votes were for sale as well as officials....

> The whole process was clear to Plato. Athens had reached the point of rejecting independence, and the freedom she now wanted was freedom from responsibility. There could be only one result.... If men insisted on being free from the burden of a life that was self-dependent and also responsible for the common good, they would cease to be free at all....

> Responsibility was the price every man must pay for freedom. It was to be had on no other terms....

> But, by that time, Athens had reached the end of freedom and was never to have it again.

Weakening of Religion: While the Pew Research Center study had found Singapore to be the world's most religiously diverse nation in 2014, the Singapore Census, which is done every 10 years, shows that the number of citizens

---

[7] Edith Hamilton, *The Echo of Greece* (New York: W.W. Norton, 1957).

who do not profess to have a religion has been increasing. The point about religion is not about the religious institution, but about the ease with which we may have a national consensus as to what are the values and behaviours which will be most beneficial for the people and the nation as a whole.

Glubb's observations are, of course, by no means predictive. But we can benefit at least by being reflective over it.

Where Do We Go From Here?

I began my lecture by explaining why Singapore was the Accidental Nation. We achieved independence, which was unplanned and unexpected. But we survived and we succeeded for 50 years.

Can our future be our conscious decision to work towards a specific strategic end?

What I have presented to you is a way to think about the future. Is the decline that Glubb writes about inevitable and unavoidable? Can we choose to make the future? Can we start again a new age of Pioneers? I think it is a choice we have. But we can keep talking and never make a choice. That would be another accident — this time of our choosing, or at least of our incapacity to choose.

I well remember my first meeting with Mr Lee Kuan Yew when he was Prime Minister and I was his Principal Private Secretary. He told me that, in the course of my work, I would be dealing with foreigners, and advised: "Always look the foreigner in his eyes. Never look down. You are dealing with him as a representative of Singapore. Conduct yourself as his equal."

As I look back, I plainly see that in this wise instruction lay the reason for what has made Singapore so much of what it is — well-regarded by the world, respected, self-aware, pushing always against the boundaries of possibilities. "Don't be weak" was never absent from Mr Lee's mind.

So where do we go from here? I began with the story of Melos, and then moved on to explain how Singapore had managed to survive and progress since independence because we paid a lot of attention to honour. We honour our word, always, by being trustworthy and dependable; and we honour each other, always, by appreciating and respecting one another, keeping the peace, and being united. And we have kept in mind this dictum: Don't be weak — externally and internally.

Finally, Glubb. The striving for affluence drove the rise of successful nations. But affluence also facilitated their fall. The rise was mostly economic; the fall was mostly social. These are the critical questions for Singapore:

- What kind of Singapore do we want in the next 10, 20, 50, 100 years?
- Can there be a way to begin a new Age of Pioneers and thereby ameliorate the effects of the Age of Decadence and Decay (extrapolating from Glubb's model in the rise and fall of nations)?

Basically, to understand why I posed the questions about the future in this way, if you could go back to Glubb's model — he talks about a country reaching its pinnacle of affluence, getting into decline — it is because the decline is mostly in social terms. The question in Singapore is whether there is a way for us to deal with social issues so that this decline is not necessarily predetermined and unavoidable. And even if they are unavoidable, can we at least ameliorate the effects? The other question is whether there is a way to deal with the future by saying "Can we go back to a new Age of Pioneers and start that cycle again?" So, at least in economic terms, is there a way to think about the future, in terms of getting back to the Age of Pioneers?

These are the questions I look forward to addressing in my next two lectures. We have reached the status of a First-World Economy. What is the First-World Society we would wish to be? What would be right for Singapore and Singaporeans, not just for the current generation but for the generations to come? In the end, it is the kind of society we want to be, and the sustainability of such a society, that are the crucial issues.

Question-and-Answer Session
Moderated by Professor Tan Tai Yong

Tan Tai Yong (TTY): Thank you, Mr Lim, for a very thoughtful, insightful and thought provoking lecture.

You argue that, by adopting the cardinal principle, "Do not be weak", Singapore has advanced from an "accidental nation" to become a successful country, whose brand name is built on trustworthiness and social peace. But you also ask, "Will this last? Can or will Singapore fall?" Using Sir John Glubb's study of the future of empires, you ask the question, "Where is Singapore now?" and "Is Singapore exhibiting signs of heading towards the Age of Decadence and Decline?" And what needs to be done to arrest the slide down, which seems inevitable once a nation-state reaches the "High Noon" of the Stage of Affluence, as most would agree Singapore is now in.

Now, Sir John Glubb wrote about empires. What about small city-states like Singapore? Small city-states will be more vulnerable, and would their trajectory be faster and shorter than large empires?

These are the questions you posed in this lecture. And I am sure many in the audience would have questions or comments for Mr Lim, so I am now going to open the session to the floor.

Participant: I have two questions. They relate to Singapore's future, our viability to defend ourselves amid a declining male population, male birth rate. I was just in reservist two months ago, and my friends and I looked at the camp, which is getting fewer and fewer people. So we joked among ourselves, "I think there are two things that we need to do: To learn how to row a *sampan*, and learn how to wave a white flag." Just joking. But the more serious question is, do you think Singapore will be able to defend itself in this climate? My second question is, do you think that, eventually, if failing to do so, we will end up re-merging with Malaysia? Thank you.

Lim Siong Guan (LSG): Your question of whether we are going to end up re-merging with Malaysia — that is always a possibility. We can never say never. But I think over a period of time, with the two countries operating in quite distinctly different kinds of ways, there will be a greater divergence with time, rather than convergence. If we expect to merge back, there must be a convergence — you cannot merge back with divergence. But whether it is possible or not, or probable or not, we cannot presume to count on it. Singapore has to figure out our way forward without thinking about that as a solution. We must seek a good solution for ourselves.

To your first question on whether Singapore can defend itself. Fundamentally, of course, we are a small place, and there is no such thing as limitless power. But the Singapore formula has been explained before as: "We need to be able to hold the ground and defend ourselves long enough for the United Nations to come in and tell everybody to stop fighting and behave themselves." That is the fundamental concept, so the question is whether Singapore can have a defence capability such that we can hold on long enough. I believe this will be possible on only one premise, and that is a massive deployment of technology.

I know that the Singapore Armed Forces works very hard on this. And may I say, just as a more general point, I think technology is "life and death" for Singapore, and maybe we have not talked of technology in such explicit terms, which we should.

As for our diminishing population, there have been observations that Singapore's fertility rate is such that no nation in the world has ever recovered from such a low rate. No nation. So, if we believe that we must preserve our culture, a certain way of thinking, a certain set of beliefs, values and behaviours that has brought us success over the years, actually, the way we are going, there is no way we can preserve it. This is not a matter of threatening people and saying, "You better pay attention." This is just seeing the data and saying, "This is a natural consequence of what happens elsewhere, and we need to have a particularly special confidence in ourselves to believe that we can avoid such an outcome."

It is just my sense that if we want to avoid the social outcomes of losing our culture, we have to think of what we can do about it. Because if we go the natural way, we will just end up with the period of decadence and decline. If we leave things to their natural outcome, we are going to lose the energy and vibrancy to rise, and to build our economy and society. So we have to ask ourselves, "Is there a way to create a new pioneering spirit, so that we can start another cycle of rise rather than simply continue with the fall?" That, to me, is the real question.

TTY: I should have stated earlier that the turnout for tonight's lecture is so good that there is a spill-over crowd. There are people watching this on video in the rooms outside, and we are also receiving questions from them. So I have got this first question coming from them: Mr Lim, if you are in your 30s again, what would you do, what organisations would you join to rejuvenate Singapore?

LSG: I like the answer that somebody provided at another forum, which was, "There are no real answers to hypothetical questions." I graduated in engineering. Perhaps, if I had understood things like these earlier, I would have paid a lot more attention to topics like history and social issues than I had. But, on the other hand, my engineering background has inclined me to always look for solutions, rather than just keep talking about concepts. You cannot have everything in life!

The question is, what would I do differently? To speak very frankly, I think I have had a very good run in the civil service. I enjoyed my time there, I felt that I had enormous opportunity to influence the direction of Singapore, the growth of Singapore, and the development of Singapore.

I feel that there is something special about the public sector, in that you can do something that benefits the whole nation. This is not to diminish the contributions of people who work in companies because, at the end of the day, companies and businesses are the real engines of growth for a country.

But whatever you do in the company is to give wealth and prosperity to the company itself. When you do something in the public sector, you are doing something for the nation as a whole.

So, if I were to relive my life, I would still choose to be in the public sector where I would actively seek to be influential in shaping the future, and doing what is good to keep the country going.

And when I speak of keeping the country going, to think in terms of three or four generations is a completely different way of thinking than if we were just thinking in terms of the next five years.

Participant: In the June 6 incident, we saw Qatar being forced by the other Gulf states into submission, after the latter alleged that it had been funding covert terrorist activities, with the US supporting Qatar's rivals, despite being a major ally of Qatar. I have a two-part question. First, what kind of repercussions do you believe such an event will have on the geopolitical dynamics and realities amongst small states? And second, would it be possible for Singapore to tweak its foreign policy to maintain its symbiotic relationship with the US, while also ensuring that it is self-reliant?

Participant: I am speaking from the perspective of a Singapore Armed Forces veteran. In my opinion, our government sells our assets away; if others impose an embargo on us, we would have no food, nothing to bring in. We sell our SingPass and all our secrets to Accenture and it invests in India. So, because we are selling things, we are looking at the bottom-line. We can be held ransom if we are selling all our assets away. So it is not about the people or defence, but how the government messes up the whole thing.

TTY: Okay, so two questions, Qatar, foreign policy, and the government.

LSG: With respect to Qatar, if you want to try to draw any parallels with Singapore, I think it is important in foreign relations to always be aware of how other people think, and what their concerns are. I think it was Lord Palmerston who said we all need to understand that, in relations between countries, there are no permanent friends, and no permanent enemies, only permanent interests. We need to be aware of other countries' permanent interests. Yes, of course, Singapore needs to maintain its independence. There are countries in the world that are independent but not sovereign; others that are sovereign but not independent. If you want to be both sovereign and independent, you have to think very carefully about how you position yourself.

In the case of Singapore, and our relations with other countries, we have to try very hard all the time to look at issues from the other country's point of view, and then we have to figure out ways by which we can be relevant to the other country. We have to ask what represents the interests of the other country, and can Singapore do something in a way that is useful to us but at the same time relevant to the other country? That is how you build up your relations with the other countries. That, really, is an abiding lesson, be it Qatar or any other country.

In my years working with Mr Lee Kuan Yew, one of the stark observations I had was that every time he was going to meet a leader of another country, he took enormous pains to discuss with a whole variety of people what the country's concerns really were, what the concerns of the leader were, and in what way Singapore could be beneficial, could be relevant to the country. It is just like, for us, when we try to maintain business relationships and social relationships, we say, "Think about the other party! What makes us a good friend or relevant to the other party?" The same thing applies to relations between countries.

As for your point about selling Singapore's assets — we can always have big arguments about whether we should sell or not, and if we decide to sell, whether we are selling at the right price or not. Some people can make the argument, for example, that it is okay to sell a power station because the power station is still in Singapore even after we have sold it. That is one way of thinking.

It is a matter of judgment as to whether indeed you are selling off your future. Sometimes, we may look at a business and conclude that if it is run by an expert in that field, it is going to yield greater economic benefits to Singapore, than if we were to try to run it ourselves. In some instances, you have to accept that the person buying up the company may have a whole international network of customers and markets which we do not have, and therefore we cannot bring that extra wealth in on our own. It is a matter of judgment whether we are better off owning the business or selling it off to someone who can create better value with it.

We may disagree sometimes with the judgment, but I would say that what the government thinks about all the time is, "Is this the right thing to do for the well-being of Singapore?" I do not think it is fair, at least from my experience and knowledge, ever to accuse the government of not caring, and of doing this or that just to get the money. I personally do not think it is true at all. That is not to say that other people looking at it may not come to a different conclusion as to what is good for Singapore. But certainly decisions of that sort are not taken lightly and are always taken with a consideration as to whether they have a longer impact on Singapore or not, or what the impact may be.

TTY: We have three questions from the room outside that deal with our youth. The first question asks, "Our youths have been brought up to be worried about competition and rankings, and therefore they take on a self-centred 'winner takes all' mind-set. So how do you inculcate in them a fighting spirit, a spirit of self-sacrifice?" The second question, from a youth leader, is: "There is a prevailing, frivolous set of values in our young, and this is creating disillusionment and eventual pursuit of cash and status. What would you advise our present young people in this context?" Finally, the third question, "The idea that the fall of nations would be caused by social issues — what are some of the key social issues you see in Singapore that are disturbing you?"

LSG: Well, I will answer the last question first, because it is the easiest to answer — come for my second lecture!

As to the questions on our youth, the wonderful thing about young people is that they are idealistic, but most of all, young people want to be involved in something which is purposeful. They want to see sense in what they are trying to do. So the much greater challenge is, how do we open up space? How do we involve our young people? How do we encourage them to take on things — initiatives which they start themselves, or, for many employers, how do you bring young people in and make them feel that they are doing something that is purposeful, that is worthwhile? This is a continual challenge. All employers need to understand that this is what they have to work at.

In my third lecture I will ask if we can go back to a new Age of Pioneers. And if we have to go back to a new Age of Pioneers, exactly what you would require is people who are willing to try new things and create new things, people who are willing to be different from others. Because if every time we want to do something, our first question is, "Who has done it elsewhere? And who has successfully done it?" — then we would have confined ourselves or condemned ourselves to being Number Two in the competition. We are uniquely different, we are uniquely small, and if we are scared to be different, that is really tragic for Singapore.

And so for the world that the young will inherit, they have to be clear that they are creating that future, and to create that future, they have to be people who are willing to try new things, willing to learn as they go, and to learn from failure. This is the challenge! And I think it can fit into what young people are really asking for and pushing for — a sense of accomplishing things. But they need to be clear. It's a world, going forward, that they have to create themselves.

To me, if we want to get into a new Age of Pioneers, we have to get out of this sense of helplessness, this sense of "it is for somebody else to decide, it is for government to do." We have to look to a world in which young people have that freedom to think for themselves and the freedom to experiment and to learn for themselves. But that requires a different mind-set. It is a mind-set of self-confidence. It is a mind-set that builds up courage. If you want to look for a new Age of Pioneers, that is where we have to go back to. It will be a brave new world for the young, which is totally possible, but they need to be clear that the future is for them to make. And it is not like, "Look at how your brother has gone ahead of you and how he has succeeded and all you need is to follow the same path." In fact, for many people, they know that the path their parents took, and the path that their older siblings are taking, is no longer a path that will give them success in the future.

Participant: You asked a question, "What kind of Singapore do we want to see in 10, 20, 50, 100 years' time?" Sometime ago, we heard a lot of talk about our declining birth rates. That does not seem to be discussed anymore. So I know that we kind of supplemented it with immigration. Then that became politically unacceptable, but I think that problem is still very real. People are still getting married less, and having fewer children. So I do not even know if Singapore will be around in 50, 100 years. That is one question.

The second question is, we hear about Artificial Intelligence and robots taking over our jobs all the time. Maybe that will address the shortage of labour because of low birth rates. I think that adds other kinds of concerns. How do you think Singapore should plan for that kind of world in the future?

LSG: Well, if Singapore dies because there are no Singaporeans, then there is not very much to worry, right? Since there are no Singaporeans to worry!

But the question is whether that is the outcome we are looking for. It is sort of saying, we must do something about it, so long as somebody else is producing the babies — but not me. No, let us recognise that low birth rate is a very serious issue. And when you talk in terms of wanting to see a future, you have to deal with the population issue, if not the birth rate issue! There has to be some adjustments there.

When I talked about what kind of Singapore we want to see 10, 20, 50 or 100 years from now, I was also thinking about something else. And this is again telling you a little bit about what is going to come out in my second lecture. I have had discussions with groups of Singaporeans who are in their 20s, 30s, 40s, and 50s, where I had asked them the question, "What kind of Singapore do you want to see 50 years from now?" The thing that really surprised me was that all four groups put at Number One, for the future they would like to see of Singapore, a "Gracious Society".

But a Gracious Society cannot be delivered by the government. If you wake up in the morning and say, "How come my neighbour does not appear to care about me?" — be aware that your neighbour is asking the same question about you! Who is going to start caring for the other first? The whole essence of a Gracious Society is the quality of the relationship amongst the citizens. That is not something the government can deliver. Do the citizens really want that? So when we say we want a Gracious Society, what are we willing to do about it?

Your next point was about robots taking over jobs and at the same time, as you say, creating new stresses in place. It will create new stresses but this is where I think our attitudes, our perspectives, need to be different. I was talking to a friend, not in Singapore, in another country. He was going around the schools setting up robotics clubs.

I asked him, "So what do you do in the robotics club?" These are nine-year-olds to 18-year-olds. He said, "First thing we do is we teach them social responsibility." Why? "Because robots must serve a good social purpose. So you go through a lesson on social responsibility." Second, he says, they take the students through lessons on how to live with failure. To me, it's terribly interesting, that he found it essential to teach the members of the robotics clubs attitudes towards life, attitudes towards work and attitudes towards others. It is not simply a matter of saying, you know, this is technology and therefore it is going to solve all problems. Because, at the end of the day, whatever you do with Artificial Intelligence (AI), when you talk about wisdom, when we talk about moral choices, AI does not do that — somebody else has to figure it out.

We need a whole openness to technology, we need to move people to see that this is a natural evolution in life and work, and they need to try to get as comfortable as they can with it. The evolving world is different from the past. But instead of simply saying, "AI is going to come and take over our jobs", we have to accept that AI is going to take over any job we do which can be brought down to formulas, and we have to move on to doing what cannot be brought down to algorithms, jobs involving the human touch, and wisdom and judgment.

This applies even to people at GIC, where I work. GIC manages the foreign reserves of Singapore. People have said that we now have more and more of these bots coming out, which even do investments. And I say, if you are investing based purely on formulas, I can guarantee you, the computer will take over your job in due course. But if you are investing in a very thoughtful kind of way, looking at how the company may move in the future, looking at how the economy may move in the future, *that* will preserve your job. But if you are doing your work simply by following a formula, your job will be gone.

So this is also the way we have to bring up our children now. Show them how to think for themselves, rather than say, all you have to do is memorise a formula and you will be okay.

TTY: I am afraid that is all the time we have for the session this evening. I want to thank Mr Lim for answering all our questions, for a delightful lecture, and to thank all of you, for coming to this lecture this evening and asking the questions.

Lecture II

THE FOURTH GENERATION

Thank you for coming to this lecture, my second in the series on the theme, "Can Singapore Fall?"

I am gratified by the many reactions to my first lecture. Contrary to what some took away from my reference to John Glubb's Age of Intellect, I am not against debate and discussion.

For Glubb, the Age of Intellect's "most dangerous by-product is the birth and growth of the notion that human intellect can solve all the problems of the world, when in fact the survival of the nation really depends on its citizens." Intellectualising is not a problem in itself, except when it stops us from taking concrete steps forward. For Singapore, the danger is if we develop a "complaint and blame" culture, where people do not bear responsibility and we end up with a deep pessimism about Singapore's future.

My preference is for us to focus on issues that involve all Singaporeans who are concerned about where our country is going. Let us reflect on what we have that should be retained, modified or abandoned, and on what we do not yet have that we should bring in. Hopefully, with an understanding of our common purpose and endeavour, more Singaporeans will decide to take action, both individually and as a nation.

This was why I accepted the S R Nathan Fellowship: it was precisely to instigate this conversation, as a call to action in the service of Singapore and our fellow Singaporeans — those here today and future generations yet unborn.

The Accidental Nation

At the close of my first lecture on "The Accidental Nation", I posed the question, **"Where Do We Go From Here?"**

I had explained why Singapore was the Accidental Nation. We had achieved independence, which was unplanned and unexpected. But we survived and we succeeded for 50 years. Now, is our future success or failure a forgone conclusion? Shall we let it be another accident depending on the natural progression of time and society? Or can we make our own future, through a conscious decision to work towards a specific strategic end?

I referred to the essay by John Glubb on *The Fate of Empires*. It is one way to think about the future. We may wonder whether Glubb's analysis of the rise and fall of empires holds lessons for small nations. Is the decline that he writes about inevitable and unavoidable? I do not believe so; it is complacency and inaction, or ill-conceived action that would make the decline inevitable and unavoidable.

Thus, I do not mean to be pessimistic at all about Singapore or Singaporeans. Those who know me know that I am often unreasonably optimistic.

I am here to say that we can and must choose to make our future. Let us see if we can start again a new Age of Pioneers, characterised by an extraordinary display of energy, courage, and innovation. It is a choice we can make, instead of falling into the trap of "NATO" — **No Action, Talk Only.**

I ought to add that Glubb was not unique in his analysis of the rise and fall of nations. In remarks that have been attributed to Alexander

Tytler, a Scottish advocate, judge, writer, and historian in the 18th century, he observed, "Great nations rise and fall. The people go from bondage to spiritual truth, to great courage, from courage to liberty, from liberty to abundance, from abundance to selfishness, from selfishness to complacency, from complacency to apathy, from apathy to dependence, from dependence back again to bondage."

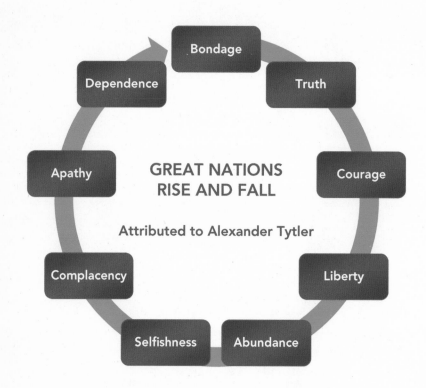

And a friend sent me "Lessons from the Ottoman", which put it even more succinctly. "Hard Times Create Strong Men; Strong Men Create Good Times; Good Times Create Weak Men; Weak Men Create Hard Times."

First-World Society

Singapore has reached the status of a First-World *Economy*. But what is the First-World *Society* we wish to be, that would be right not just for the current generation but also for the generations to come? This is the crucial issue here.

We should think of this in two ways. First, what would be good for the future, not simply what would be convenient or comforting for us today, but what would be good for our children, grandchildren, and great grandchildren, so that Singapore would still be the best place for them — we will never be perfect, but we can be the place where they can make the best of their talents and abilities. Second, our thinking should be oriented towards action; to talk by way of assigning blame and passing responsibility for action to others is one way, but to talk with a view of refining ideas that lead to us taking action would be a better way.

Singapore in 50 Years

What kind of Singapore do we want in the next 10, 20, 50, 100 years? To help us concentrate our minds, let me specifically pose the question as, "What is the Singapore we would like to see (if we were still alive then) when SG100 comes around?"

We could take the attitude that SG100 will happen anyway — just be patient and wait. But this could then simply be a case where, "To wait and see is to wait and die." Let us honour ourselves by choosing deliberately.

SG100 will be the time of the fourth generation of Singaporeans since independence in 1965, if we count one generation for every 25 years. For many of the young people in the audience, it is not the generation of your children or even your grandchildren. It is the generation of your great grandchildren.

You may find it ludicrous to think of Singapore in 50 years when no one can even be clear what the future would be like in 10 years. But if we think that way, then we are thinking in a reactive mode, where we need to know a situation before we can think of what to do. This is the mental posture of the hopeless and helpless. We must refuse to be that. We should be thinking of a future we can shape and create, even though we may be small as a country,

> Our thinking should be oriented towards action; to talk by way of assigning blame and passing responsibility for action to others is one way, but to talk with a view of refining ideas that lead to us taking action would be a better way.

and subject to events and developments in the world that are often beyond our control.

Last November, I had the privilege of helping in a workshop of more than 60 young people in their 20s and early 30s, to address the question, "What kind of Singapore would you like to see in 50 years? Describe it in five phrases at most." The "five phrases" rule was to ensure focus so that there can be a concentration of effective effort, yet not so narrow as to force a limited view. The workshop divided its participants into groups of six or seven, each group discussing amongst themselves, and finally agreeing on what they considered to be the five most important characteristics of the Singapore they wished for in 50 years. We then put up all the ideas from the groups, clustering similar ideas together. Next, we gave every participant five votes to select the five ideas that most appealed to them individually.

The top five ideas the participants selected were:

1. Gracious Society: Doing the right thing even when no one is watching
2. Beyond Academics: Focus on character and passion
3. Active Ageing: Focus on those in their 30s and 40s (physical and mental health)
4. Beyond Geographic Advantage: Focus on innovation and e-commerce
5. More Sensitive and Tolerant People: Focus on values

I do not know how you feel about this, but I was both encouraged and inspired. And I note again that these were young people in their 20s and early 30s.

The year before, in 2015, I had met two groups of labour movement leaders. They were mostly in their 40s and 50s. One of the questions posed was, "What kind of Singapore would you like to have in 50 years?" These were their top seven wishes:

1. Gracious Society
2. Work-Life balance
3. Innovative/ creative/ smart Singapore
4. Singapore as an economic leader
5. Jobs availability/ security

6. Safe and secure
7. Clean and green

I found it quite remarkable, that in the small groups of Singaporeans I met in their 20s, 30s, 40s and 50s, the top wish for their grandchildren and great grandchildren was for Singapore to be a Gracious Society.

Each of us can undertake our own exercise of asking ourselves what kind of Singapore we should like to see when SG100 comes along. I spent an afternoon thinking it over for myself. This is my list:

- A Singapore that continues to succeed despite our smallness
- Racial, religious and community synergy
- A Gracious Society
- Children proud of their parents
- Citizens proud of their country

Perhaps all of us should spend time in groups to think over SG100, and what we can and should do to influence the outcome.

Kampung Spirit

Let me explore further this wish for a Gracious Society. Perhaps the more colloquial term is "Kampung Spirit" — if we think of it as something that we perhaps once had and have since mostly lost.

I have a friend in Penang who remarked to me, "You guys in Singapore talk about Kampung Spirit. Do you know what it means? During Chinese New Year, my father gives out *ang pows* to his grandchildren, who all line up eagerly to receive their yearly collection. Many children in the neighbourhood, including the Malay and Indian children, also line up and duly get their *ang pows*. Would Singaporeans who want the Kampung Spirit do likewise?"

In Singapore's busy city life, this Kampung Spirit is also in the motor-cyclist who stops in the rain to check up on you when your car has stalled by the roadside, or to help clear the traffic for an ambulance during rush hour. So there are still instances of this here. Indeed, they are often reported on. Perhaps because we do not yet have a deep culture of graciousness, each of these incidents becomes worthy news in itself. To make the point more personal, some of us might leave our home each morning and wonder, "How come my neighbour does not appear to care about me and my family?" Well, we can be sure our neighbours are asking the same question about us. Who is going to start this process of care and concern for our neighbour?

National Values

To get some sense of Singaporeans' idea of the Kampung Spirit, let me refer you to a survey of national values that was conducted from March to June 2015 by aAdvantage Consulting, a consulting firm in Singapore, together with the Barrett Values Centre of the UK. The 2015 survey is the latest in the series, which is conducted every three years. The survey used an international survey instrument, which has been applied in many countries around the world. Respondents are shown a list of values and behaviours, and asked to pick items from the list that they consider the most important for themselves. Then, *from the same list*, they are asked to pick the values and behaviours they see in others around them. Finally, and again *from the same list*, they are asked to pick what they desire for the future.

The top 10 values and behaviours the respondents in Singapore picked as representing what they considered to be the most important for themselves were, in descending order of priority:

1. Family
2. Responsibility
3. Friendship
4. Happiness
5. Health
6. Caring
7. Honesty
8. Compassion
9. Positive attitude
10. Respect

It is a highly commendable list and we all should be proud of it. Of the 10 items, I would say only one clearly involves the government, namely, health, which perhaps is something like 50 per cent personal responsibility and 50 per cent government provision. All the others involve personal attitudes and behaviour.

Next — bearing in mind the respondents were choosing items from the same list — the top 10 values and behaviours they saw in others around them were, in descending order:

1. *Kiasu* (Being concerned about losing out)
2. Competitive
3. Materialistic
4. Self-centred
5. *Kiasi* (Being concerned about dying or losing out completely)
6. Blame
7. Security
8. Education opportunities
9. Effective healthcare
10. Peace

I grant that the last four items — Security, Education opportunities, Effective healthcare and Peace — are principally the responsibility of the government. But the first six items — *Kiasu*, Competitive, Materialistic, Self-centred, *Kiasi* and Blame — reflect the life attitudes of individuals.

Before exploring Singapore's situation further, we should note that the corresponding lists of what the current values are like in the United States and the United Kingdom, for example, come out quite differently from the Singapore list, though the data available for them are a little outdated.

The top 10 items reflecting current culture in the US in 2011 were:

1. Blame
2. Bureaucracy
3. Wasted resources
4. Corruption
5. Materialistic
6. Uncertainty about the future
7. Conflict/ aggression

8. Crime/ violence
9. Unemployment
10. Short-term focus

And for the UK, the top 10 items reflecting current culture in 2012 were:

1. Bureaucracy
2. Crime/violence
3. Uncertainty about the future
4. Corruption
5. Blame
6. Wasted resources
7. Media influence
8. Conflict/ aggression
9. Drugs/ alcohol
10. Apathy

The Singapore list of *Kiasu*, Competitive, Materialistic, Self-centred, *Kiasi*, Blame, Security, Education opportunities, Effective healthcare, and Peace is so different and, in many ways, more positive than that of the US and UK. Nevertheless, the interesting question is, why is it that what is *perceived in Singapore society* is so different from what the survey respondents said were their *personal values*: Family, Responsibility, Friendship, Happiness, Health, Caring, Honesty, Compassion, Positive Attitude, and Respect? These are what Singaporeans say are most important for them. So if everyone is saying these are the most important, the interesting question is, how it is that they are not seeing these values demonstrated around them? If the personal values were actually lived out, we should reasonably expect that at least some of these values would be reflected in a description of current culture. But, at least in 2015, not a single one of the personal values was reflected in the prevailing culture as perceived by the respondents.

One possible explanation for the incongruence is that the list of personal values did not reflect the truth because respondents wanted to present a positive image of themselves. But there is a second fascinating possible explanation: both the lists are honest and true. The most important value for the individual is "family", so, because *my* family is the most important; I would cut queues for the sake of *my* family. I would argue with my daughter's teacher because *my* family is most important, and so on. Others may see my behaviour as *kiasu*, whereas all I am doing is living out my belief that family — *my* family — is most important to me. You can decide for yourself what the correct explanation is.

As for what they desired for the future, respondents in the Singapore survey listed the following as their top 10 items:

1. Affordable housing
2. Caring for the elderly
3. Effective healthcare
4. Compassion
5. Quality of life
6. Caring for the disadvantaged
7. Peace
8. Employment opportunities
9. Caring for the environment
10. Concern for future generations

A cynical view would be that practically all the items are for the government to do. The future that is desired is for the government to do it all, almost.

When Singapore attained internal self-government in 1959 and then independence in 1965, we can say there were virtually only four critical deliverables for the government, namely, jobs, homes, education and health. Jobs were created through industrialisation and a supremely welcoming environment for foreign investment spearheaded by the Economic Development Board. Homes were built by the Housing and Development Board (HDB) and financed for individual ownership through the Central Provident Fund system, where many homeowners could pay off their mortgages without having to top up from their monthly income. Education, particularly to create futures for the children, was met with massive expansion of school places. And health was delivered in the form of basic healthcare, as the population was still young.

But looking at the list of desires for the future, can the government really deliver on all the items listed by the survey respondents, despite the best of its intentions? Desires today are a lot more varied than in the 1960s. Can the government meet them all? Is creating the society and country that Singaporeans desire, something more for citizens to help themselves on than for the government to dictate and supply?

Hidden Wealth of Nations

David Halpern, in his book, *The Hidden Wealth of Nations*, observed, "Richer nations are happier than poor nations, yet decades of economic growth does not seem to have increased the happiness within them…. This paradox is explained by 'the hidden wealth of nations' — the extent to which citizens get along with others independently drives both economic growth and well-being."

In short, there is a critical hidden wealth of nations that lies in the quality of relationships among its citizenry. Does this premise hold for Singapore too?

The CIA World Factbook 2017 lists Singapore as having the seventh highest GDP per capita in the world. I suspect Halpern would be correct that Singaporeans would not be happier even if Singapore should become the country with the highest GDP per capita in the world. It would seem that there is something instinctive when Singaporeans in their 20s, 30s, 40s and 50s all say that the most important characteristic of Singapore, which they would like to see in 50 years, is a Gracious Society, not economic success, though I am sure they were all assuming a continuance of good economic standards of living. But how practical would it be to expect an outcome of a Gracious Society, given the survey of national values I mentioned earlier, which found the dominant perceived cultural characteristics of Singapore to be *Kiasu*, Competitive, Materialistic, Self-centred, *Kiasi*, and Blame?

The most critical observation we have to make about Gracious Society, or Kampung Spirit, is that it reflects the state of relations among individual citizens. In other words, this is not an outcome the government can produce. **The government can encourage and facilitate, but Gracious Society is something we the citizens have to deliver ourselves.** Can we do it? Do we want to do it? Is it important enough? **While the Singapore we** wanted in its first 50 years may have been defined in economic terms, it is rather clear that the future Singapore we want in our next 50 years ought to be also defined in social terms, without neglecting the economic wherewithal to maintain our living standards.

Our practical Singaporeans might say, Gracious Society is nice to have — but does it have to be the top priority now? Is it really urgent? My view is that **we** *can* **only get there if we think in terms of a change that happens over a generation — and because it** is a long-term outcome, it requires conviction, tenacity, and action *now*. Even though little money would be required, the heart and the mind must want it almost as a "life and death" issue.

The most critical observation we have to make about Gracious Society, or Kampung Spirit, is that it reflects the state of relations among individual citizens. In other words, this is not an outcome the government can produce. The government can encourage and facilitate, but Gracious Society is something we the citizens have to deliver ourselves.

A Gracious Society could be exactly the kind of antidote to the social degradation and national decay that Glubb finds to afflict nations, both large and small, once they reach high levels of affluence. But let us first think about what a Gracious Society would be like, so that we can have a clearer idea of whether we want it, and whether we can get to it.

What a Gracious Society Can Look Like

Often when people think of Gracious Society, their minds imagine the displaced and the handicapped, the poor and the misfits, and how those groups of people should be taken care of. But Gracious Society, or Kampung Spirit, is really about the countless little interactions between neighbours and everyone else we mix with or have to work with every day of the week. It is the little things that define culture and the reality of society.

I know there are already many initiatives for people to help one another and be kind to one another. There have been many occasions where people reach out to help others in trouble. This gives us optimism that in a crisis, people will not simply think of themselves and their families, but will extend their hearts and hands to those around them. But what I am advocating is graciousness as a part of our character as a nation, not just episodic acts of kindness. This is culture — an integral part of our make-up as a people.

Honour (Singapore)

I am the Founding Chairman of Honour (Singapore), a charity whose mission is the promotion of a culture of honour and honouring for the well-being of the nation. The impetus for founding Honour (Singapore) was SG50 — my conviction that SG50 should not just be about celebration, but should be a time of reflection as to how Singapore had managed to survive and succeed since independence. Honour (Singapore) is multi-racial and multi-religious in its perspective, doing what it can to enhance the well-being of the country for the benefit of all.

One of our major projects is sponsoring young filmmakers to produce short films on the theme of honouring the "invisible people". These are the people who serve us and do good for us day after day, but whose presence and service we often fail to register or acknowledge. The invisible people are the bus drivers, the lift attendants, the "aunty" in the office keeping the place clean, and the domestic helpers. We have films on our website, www.honour.sg, giving honour to the SMRT technician, ex-prisoners, the undertaker, our first women Olympians, nurses, firemen, a family with a member who has Down's Syndrome, and many more.

Let me show you an example with the film entitled, *Ayah*, which features an SMRT technician who is dedicated to his duties, but whose daughter at first misunderstood him as not appreciating her efforts for his birthday. You can find the film on our website under the tab, "Short Films".[1]

If we open our eyes and our hearts to the world around us each day, we can see a lot that is worthy of our honour, care, and support.

Someone described to me a situation in Japan where, at the end of lunch, he was asked if he would like to have coffee. Yes, he would like to

---

[1] Watch the film at this link: http://honour.sg/portfolio/ayah/.

have coffee, but he found that all his Japanese friends at the lunch decided not to. They later explained to him that they had noticed that other people were waiting for tables to clear so that they could have their turn at lunch, so his friends decided the right thing to do was to release their table as quickly as possible, thus declining coffee.

Another person told me about his experience in climbing the Sydney Harbour Bridge with a group that included several Japanese. At the end of the climb, everyone was given a towel to wipe off their sweat. But he saw that the Japanese also used their towel to wipe the safety gear the group had been equipped with. They were doing it in consideration of the next group who would be making the climb.

I remember flying to Tokyo and being picked up by a chauffeur arranged by my sponsors in Japan. After helping me to get to the carpark with my luggage, he told me to wait at the kerbside, and proceeded to *run* to the car. This was his expression of considerate service.

I also recall taking a walk in the Japanese countryside. *Every* child and *every* adult I came across freely greeted me, "*konnichiwa*" — the Japanese informal greeting for "Good day!" They would not have known that I was not Japanese, but the earnestness and spontaneity of their greeting was spirit-lifting.

Allow me just one more example from Japan. A friend told me that his wife made a point of sweeping the road in front of their home with the help of her children. He assured me that this was not unusual; it was simply doing something they had grown up with — looking after the neighbourhood and helping to maintain a clean environment.

I apologise that all my examples come from Japan. I think that Japanese culture, nurtured in children from young, fosters social consideration and responsibility, and a way of looking out for others. I refer to Japan not to urge everyone to become Japanese cultural clones, but to show that it is possible to have a social environment where people feel a sense of being recognised and being treated with respect and consideration. These are the little day-to-day things that we can all do if we care to look beyond our own immediate needs, and actually notice others and their needs. We can learn to see anew and act; we can get to a Gracious Society if we think it is important enough.

Singapore has had our Courtesy Campaign in the past, which has since been absorbed into the Singapore Kindness Movement. Can we do more? *Should* we do more? Can we get to being a Gracious Society faster?

Caring about others and doing good is basically a matter of the heart. This is not about religion; it is about beliefs and values and morals and ethics, which may come from religion, or a personal study of civilisation and culture, or simply the way we have been brought up. Indeed, our disappointment and frustration are particularly great with those who claim to be religious but do not live up to their religious precepts of caring and doing good. All religions teach virtually the same social mores of good and right, and there are many atheists and agnostics who practise the same standards out of the goodness of their hearts or something deep within them in their consciences, which tell them what is good and what is bad, what is right and what is wrong.

Start With the Young, Start With the Parents

The Chinese have a saying, "三岁定终身" (sān suì dìng zhōng shēn), which means, "At the age of three you can know what one will be like for the rest of his life." What a remarkable statement drawn from thousands of years of Chinese civilisation! Three years old is before the kid even turns up in nursery, not to mention kindergarten or Primary One. The lesson is plain: parents and the child's earliest environment hold the key to the behaviours the child will display towards others as they grow up, and their attitude towards life and work in adulthood. Speaking to teachers of children in the lower primary levels, I found that many of them feel that what they have to do — often with

Developing a whole culture and value system starts from the home, and is then reinforced by the school and society. This process may well take a generation, so we have to start *now*, building upon what has been done in the past, but moving in a far more deliberate, urgent, and holistic manner.

limited success — is to undo the damage that the parents have caused at home, from what they had done or failed to do.

If three years old seems much too young for you, you could take comfort from a saying of the Jesuits, an order in the Catholic Church. They say, "Give me a child till seven and I will give you the man." In other words, they believe that a child can be moulded for life within seven years.

Whether we decide to take the word of the Chinese of old or the Jesuits, the point simply is that parents and the family have the most fundamental of responsibilities in guiding and shaping the child before they get to kindergarten or school. I am speaking here of values and attitudes, which are more *caught* by example than *taught* by instruction in our young.

So how should we think if we were to take Glubb's observations seriously? His study indicated that the push for affluence brought economic wealth and political power to nations. But affluence subsequently also catalysed nations' decadence and decline. What we would like to explore is whether Singapore could think of a way to ameliorate the weakening of the nation, and inspire a new pioneering spirit for growth and well-being. Singaporeans seem to agree that we want a Gracious Society. But developing a whole culture and value system starts from the home, and is then reinforced by the school and society. This process may well take a generation, so we have to start *now*, building upon what has been done in the past, but moving in a far more deliberate, urgent, and holistic manner.

Maslow's Hierarchy of Needs

Am I promoting naïve altruism when I suggest that Singaporeans think and care about others as a way of life? Far from it. I think it can in fact be more like enlightened self-interest.

I am sure most of you would have heard of Maslow's Hierarchy of Needs. When I ask my audiences how many needs there are in the hierarchy, I get responses like five, six, or seven. Often, people are not sure. But when I ask them what is the highest need identified by Maslow, everyone knows it is Self-Actualisation. Everyone. Of course everyone can remember that because it is all about yourself; whether it is four, five, six, it does not matter! We can all remember what is most important to ourselves.

Well, Abraham Harold Maslow (1908–1970) was an American psychologist who hypothesised that the needs of human beings lie in a hierarchy, where once one level of needs is met, the next higher level of needs gains prominence. He identified five levels of needs:

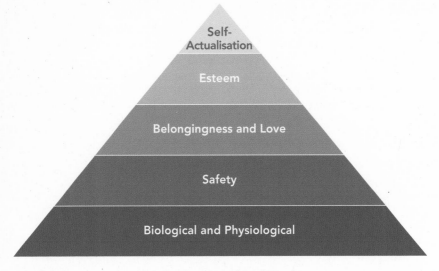

Maslow's Hierarchy of Needs

1. Biological and Physiological needs (food, air, water, shelter, etc.)
2. Safety needs (security, stability, law, etc.)
3. Belongingness and Love needs (family, friends, etc.)
4. Esteem needs (status, reputation, achievement, etc.)
5. Self-Actualisation needs (the realisation of one's potential, etc.)

However, further research in the field concluded that Maslow's list is incomplete, and that human beings have three more needs:

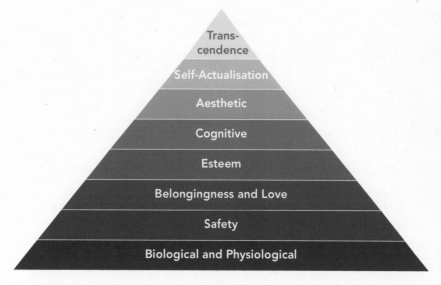

Maslow's Hierarchy of Needs (Extended)

6. Cognitive needs (understanding, etc.)
7. Aesthetic needs (beauty, balance, form, etc.)
8. Transcendence needs (helping others realise their potential)

It turns out that the highest need we all have is the need for transcendence. That is, the need to move beyond just thinking of ourselves, to thinking of others and helping them reach their personal growth and self-fulfilment. Transcendence is ranked as the highest of all needs in the human psyche. To put it simply, if we want to live a full life, we have to remember that it is not about ourselves, but about others.

Certainly not everyone would agree with Maslow's five needs or even the extended list of eight. But I believe that most of us derive an enormous sense of satisfaction and fulfilment when we do something good for someone else, enjoying their gratitude and having the smile in their eyes warm our hearts. Serving beyond ourselves is what gives each of us meaning and a deep sense of purpose in life and achievement.

But a Gracious Society is not just about giving. It is not about "giving until it hurts". Certainly, it is not naïvely dealing with people who say "give and take" but who really mean, "you give, I take!"

For giving to be possible, there must also be a "receiver". Sometimes, we need to be the receiver so that someone can be a "giver". I have a friend who is older than me and he tells me that, often, when he rides the train, some youngster would offer his or her seat. He used to turn down the offer, saying he only needed to go a short distance and therefore could stand. The youngster often looked embarrassed that his or her offer had been turned down.

One day, my friend had an epiphany and from then on, he accepted the offer of a seat, even when he only had one station to go. This allowed him to give the youngster his good deed and happiness for the day. So my friend has come up with an aphorism: When you are young, you get happiness by giving with good grace and humility; when old, you get happiness by accepting with good grace and humility.

More for SG100

I have spoken much about a Gracious Society. Let me go back to the other items on the list that came out from my meeting with the young Singaporeans last year. These were:

1. Beyond Academics: Focus on character and passion
2. Active Ageing: Focus on 30s and 40s (physical and mental health)
3. Beyond Geographic Advantage: Focus on innovation and e-commerce
4. More Sensitive and Tolerant People: Focus on values

The last item, More Sensitive and Tolerant People, links back to a Gracious Society. I will address Beyond Geographic Advantage, in my next lecture. Active Ageing is partly related to demographics, which I will also take up in my next lecture, and partly related to social and personal well-being, which all of us should take to heart in a Gracious Society. I shall now discuss the item, Beyond Academics: Focus on character and passion.

Character

Character establishes the trustworthiness of the individual. We all know how critical character is in life and work. That is how we choose our friends. Can we trust them with our secrets and to look out for us? This is also how we choose who to promote in the workplace — we judge whether we can trust them to always do their best and act in the interest of the organisation.

Universities and schools see much of their role as sharing knowledge and developing skills, rather than guiding their students towards succeeding in work and life. Those of us who lead organisations know that what we look for when we recruit or promote people is not just competence and experience; we also look for trustworthiness and dependability.

We ask: Will they do their best according to their talents and capabilities? Will they observe deadlines, and let us know if they will not be able to meet the deadlines? We also wonder whether our people will cooperate, collaborate and support one another. Can we trust our people in their attitude towards their work? Will they look out for one another and function as family or as a team?

Universities and schools often fail to make the point with their students that, to succeed in work and life, they need to be *trustworthy*, and not just competent in their skills and abilities.

Trust is the most important currency for long-term relationships. We all know this instinctively. Trust is both critical and essential in relationships with parents and family, friends and colleagues, subordinates and bosses, business partners and customers, and with government and the community.

Passion

As for passion, in all competition, the person or organisation with the most energy and imagination always wins. This demands passion — a total commitment to the cause. The Singapore of the future needs to pay a lot more attention to the drive and determination of individuals. We need to value character and passion — soul and spirit — beyond academic results and skills certificates.

Maximal Development of Talents and Abilities

In addition to character and passion, there is the need for maximal development of the talents and abilities of individual Singaporeans. Unlike the Gracious Society where the government should facilitate but cannot deliver, because the quality of relationship between citizens can only be delivered by individual citizens, this is something for the government to do with the support of parents and the active involvement of individuals themselves.

The government should seek to create an environment where every Singaporean has maximum opportunity to be what they can be according to their talents and abilities. The greater attention to early childhood education is a critical move in this direction. The whole education system should be targeted at identifying and developing the talents and abilities of every Singaporean, while the work and social environment should provide the most supportive conditions for this. Parents are a critical part of such a national exercise, because they are the ones who shape the character and life attitudes of the child before the child even turns up in kindergarten. But the critical actor is each individual, his/ her sense of honouring his/ her own individual talents and abilities, and contributing in a way that reflects responsibility towards self, family, and nation.

But for this to be possible, a fundamental change in our attitude is needed. We must stop focusing on shortcomings and weaknesses, and instead focus on strengths and abilities. Stop looking at people as handicapped or imperfect — look instead for what they can do well. The autistic, the dyslexic, the polio victim, and the person with one hand or foot — we have to support and help each seek to discover what they are able to do. Stop thinking in terms of disabilities, and start thinking of *people* who possess "differ-abilities" — different abilities. This demands a different perspective on the part of parents, teachers, employers, society and government. They — and we — are not burdens to bear or problems to solve, but possibilities we have to discover. It is an integral part of being a Gracious Society.

Gracious Society — Nothing Less

The Fourth Generation will hopefully have much to celebrate at SG100. But we cannot simply leave it to them to make the Singapore of their time for themselves. Certainly, many things they can, and should, do for themselves. Each generation must solve its own problems. But some things require the work of a generation or more to bring about. For these, we must start work on now, to be in time for that future. A Gracious Society is such a thing. It would be a society that makes Singapore stand out from the rest of the world. It would be a Singapore that draws out, and benefits from what David Halpern has identified as the "hidden wealth of nations".

A Gracious Society, because of its spirit of other-centredness, can help to induce better relationships among people and the different sectors of society, including organisations and the government. There is scope for the public sector to exercise greater sensitivity towards the people in its communications. Similarly, there can be greater attention to employee engagement in businesses and organisations, better service to customers, and greater instinctive concern for issues like income and socioeconomic divides. Our highly educated Gen X, Gen Y — the Millennials, and the incoming Gen Z — the Centennials, all offer us much hope. Every generation ultimately seeks meaning and purpose. Our youths are no different: they want to do good, but they also need their own space and the scope to discover their talents and abilities. Parents, bosses, and mentors can do more to support and encourage our youths on their life's work and journey.

A Gracious Society is one where people feel good because others care, where we flourish together because we each can be the best we can be by helping ourselves, and helping one another. We can start today to build a First-World Society that our Fourth Generation will be proud of, and benefit from, because we have moved in our generation to lay the groundwork for them to flourish and prosper 50 years later. By that time, and hopefully earlier, whenever any Singaporean or Singapore resident thinks of "SG", they will also think, "GS" — Gracious Society!

Question-and-Answer Session
Moderated by Kuik Shiao-yin

Kuik Shiao-yin (KSY): Thank you for the great speech, Mr Lim. My first reaction to this lecture was, "How old will I actually be at SG100?" I just turned 40 and last week, my daughter just turned three. So that would make me 88 years old, and she would be 51.

That made me reflect on two big things that you brought up. First, there was a strong theme of graciousness. Grace makes me think of something that is freely given, unmerited, and is particularly striking when it is extended to the powerless from someone who is powerful. You also talked a lot about how it is the role and responsibility of the citizen to build up this culture of care and concern; the government can only facilitate it and not do anything else.

So, one of the questions I wanted to pose is, what exactly does it mean for the government to facilitate a culture of grace? Is it possible for policy to be written in a way that facilitates or models grace and graciousness, or do you believe that it cannot be done?

Lim Siong Guan (LSG): As an example of how the government can facilitate relationship between citizens, I note developments by the HDB — they are building the new estates in a way that facilitates interaction. They are creating more common spaces. Nevertheless, despite such moves, people might come together and yet just go to their own stall or shop, do their own thing, and then go back home without interacting with others.

Thus, on the quality of relationships, the government can create the conditions in its design of physical space. The People's Association now has this movie bus that goes around to show movies at Community Centres. One might say, "Well, you know, at the end of the day, it even requires the People's Association to create such a night out; people come, they enjoy the movies." But the question is, how can this become more naturally the way people interact with one another?

I imagine that there would be instances where, when people physically live closer to one another, they are drawn further apart socially. This is, in fact, an effect of urbanisation.

And there could be parents who tell their children not to mix with other kids in the neighbourhood, in case they end up quarrelling. The intention might be that, the less interaction we have, the less chance there will be that we end up quarrelling. But the fact of the matter is that, the less interaction you have, the more the chances that any quarrel that you might have will become a really big quarrel, simply because of misunderstanding and an inadequate understanding of each other.

So, yes, the government can facilitate a Gracious Society, if they agree that it creates a good kind of social grease, which brings with it "social competitive advantage", an enhancing of social capital. The government can facilitate social capital on a national basis, not just at the level of small communities. If the government agrees, then this is really about asking, each time you think of a policy, are you helping to reinforce or are you detracting from a Gracious Society?

So, we must first agree that that is what we want, and what is important for Singapore going forward. Because, if we do not agree, we are never going to do it. But if we do, then you find this running through the whole way — whether it is government or business or any organisation or the family, going down to the individual, and each action will reinforce the other.

But I agree with your first point on whether we are prepared to be the initiator. I think, very often, people say, "Well, if my neighbour is kind to me, I will be kind to them, but they need to be kind to me first." Well, your neighbour is saying exactly the same thing, which is why graciousness does not start. So, what you say about grace being something you offer is true. Indeed, this is why it comes down to the responsibility of each person.

KSY: I would imagine that one of the pushbacks to this statement, "The government can only facilitate, but it cannot produce it" would be, "How can the government then model grace to its people or citizenry?"

LSG: Let me tell you my feelings on this. If we take the idea of Gracious Society as being a part of our national culture, I think public servants will think more about the people they are serving. They will take more initiative and action, instead of just saying, "Fill up a form."

If, as a people, we become more oriented towards graciousness, I believe it will have its effect on the way government policies are developed, the way government services are delivered, and the way people look out for one another.

KSY: You associated the culture of graciousness with the Kampung Spirit, right? One of the pushbacks that we normally hear from young people is that Kampung Spirit means nothing to them, because Kampung just has no emotional resonance. Do you feel that when you interact with the younger generation today, the Kampung Spirit is not there? Or do you think it is simply different?

LSG: Well, the only reason I used the term Kampung Spirit is because so many people are using it. But what about young people? I believe young people are looking for companionship; they are looking for good fun and fellowship with one another.

I believe being together in a community is very important to young people — especially when families have become smaller, this has become even more important for those who have tasted what it is like to have close friends and what it is like to be doing things together.

In my observation, what is possibly a bit missing is young people taking the initiative to do things; instead, they may wait for it to be done for them or to them first, before responding. But I am very optimistic about our young people, because I think graciousness is really an important need in their lives. That is why I talked about Maslow's Hierarchy going up to the eighth level where our most important need as human beings is transcendence, a looking out for the good of others.

Participant: I have some questions leftover from the last lecture, and some new questions — three questions altogether.

LSG: I think you have to give an opportunity to other people, so just choose the most important of the three questions.

Participant: I will finish in two minutes.

The first is about political systems. I think that the US Constitution is an exceptional document, with principles and ideals that are wise and timeless; it has proven to be respected and the leaders' actions are shaped or constrained by it, and I find that it serves America well. What are your thoughts about Singapore going towards constitutionalism, rather than the current model of parliamentary supremacy?

The second question is on our education system. In late September, Deputy Prime Minister Mr Tharman Shanmugaratnam spoke about reforms in our education system. In these reforms, he clearly and objectively highlighted that it is the admissions system that needs critical reform. Many young people are actually going overseas to study, or like in my case, not being able to afford to go overseas, end up doing distance learning; in some other cases, they totally give up on getting a university education. So, what are your thoughts about legislating opportunities?

The third question relates to the soul of Singapore. Before Mr George Yeo left the Cabinet, he spoke about the struggle for Singapore's soul; I will read a very short part of what he said:

> Dear Singaporeans, this has been a struggle for the soul of Singapore. We need a bigger heart to embrace all Singaporeans. This has to be a unity, a unity based on greater diversity. At the heart of the government is the PAP, but we need a PAP that will listen and listen carefully. A PAP that talks with and not at, a PAP that is not perceived as arrogant or high-handed. We need a transformed PAP.

So what are your thoughts? How do you think Singapore is faring and what are the areas you think we can actually improve in?

KSY: That is quite a lot to answer!

Participant: I kept my promise, two minutes!

LSG: To your last question quoting George Yeo, I agree completely with everything he says. You asked me for my thoughts about how Singapore is faring: quite frankly, my thoughts are irrelevant. Because if I express them and you agree with me, then that is fine. If I express my thoughts and you disagree with me, I will accept the fact that your thoughts and judgments are as valid as mine. And so, my thoughts on this are an irrelevant point.

What is relevant here, however, is our expectations of a good government. Is the current government delivering and providing good government? That is the critical question and every Singaporean is going to make his or her own judgment about it. So, I think what George Yeo mentions is very relevant; in a way, his message is for the PAP itself, and it is really for the PAP to decide how much of it they want to take up.

At the end of the day, I think we have to ask ourselves, "What is the job of government?" In my simplistic way of thinking, the job of government is to do the things that individual citizens cannot do. The starting point has to be that individual citizens should be given as much freedom as can possibly be given while maintaining order in society for the benefit of all.

There are things that individual citizens cannot deliver on their own, and so they need to contract it to a body that can take on this bigger function. Things like running an armed forces or police force, maintaining order in the streets — the individual citizen cannot do it without creating a whole lot of disorder. We have to keep asking, "At what point does the individual need to take into account the fact that there is a limit to the way they exercise their freedom, especially if and when it starts to impinge on the ability of their neighbours to similarly exercise their freedom?" It is a fine judgment, and the government may oftentimes get it right, but sometimes gets it wrong. At the end of the day, people should also have the opportunity to say what they think the government has done well and what it has not done so well.

Once upon a time, people only had the ability to exercise their views once every five or so years when they went for the General Elections. Now, they can express their views within five seconds through social media! People welcome social media, saying, "Social media is the mechanism by which you can speak truth to power." But now the big challenge we have is how to speak truth to social media. There is so much fake news that this has become a big challenge on its own. Nevertheless, social media is indeed a mechanism that speaks truth to power, and by which we can offer feedback.

Going back to your first question about the US system, I will just say this: I think there is no other country in the world in the same position as Singapore is. At the end of the day, we have to exercise our own judgement as to what makes the most sense for the way we are, rather than just say, "Look at the US system." Maybe that is a system that can run for a big country; it is a system where, as you said, there is constitutionality, with checks and balances, but just remember — continuous checks and balances also means that you have a system where it can be very difficult to change anything. As an example, of how different Singapore is, the US economy is so large that you can expect the market economy to yield proper pricing through competition. In a good number of instances, such a system is not feasible for Singapore, simply because the small size of our economy does not allow the degree of competition necessary to yield good pricing. Then we need the government to come in and do a lot more by way of regulation than you would do in a big economy, where competitors can check one another.

With regard to the political system, let me say this. At the end of the day, each country has to decide what is best for itself. You may have a view that moving away from what we have is a great idea, but you also have to think in terms of what you gain and what you lose by it. We must be open all the time to change, and to be able to change in an urgent way where conditions demand it. But I think, just looking at what other people are doing, and saying, "Let us do the same as them" is a very dangerous way of thinking about change. As Singapore, we ought to learn from everywhere in the world, but we have to think for ourselves.

As for your point about the education system and legislating opportunities and so forth — I mentioned in my speech that I believe that the government must have a frame of mind that says we want to develop the talents and abilities of every Singaporean to the best of our ability, rather than looking at, say, people with disabilities and saying, "There is a problem." No, I do not think we should look at it in terms of there being a problem, but in terms of what talents and abilities we have to try to discover, and to try to create the conditions under which those with particular disabilities would be able to contribute according to what they are able to do.

So what can we do in this regard? Let us first recognise that some of these issues do require interventions that cost significant money. We are making progress as a country. But remember that we can talk this way because our country already has a reasonable level of quality of life and a reasonable level of affluence.

Let us get our principles right first. I would like to see the government working with parents, to try to help develop every Singaporean's talents and abilities to the best extent possible; after that, the rest really has to be up to the individual. What are you going to contribute in your own life? I hope that people will think in terms of what they can contribute to the nation for the benefit of Singaporeans as a whole.

In my next lecture, I will talk about how we can best prepare our people for the future even though we do not know what the next 10 years is going to be like. I will, for example, speak of the need to adjust our thinking on innovation. We have to move away from this idea that, "We want to be innovative, but only recognise and applaud people when they have got the gold medal." We are going to have to put a lot more emphasis on effort and on whether people have tried their best.

In the future, I think a lot more is going to depend on the person's attitude, motivation, and imagination, rather than just acquiring skills as the end goal. The responsibility of each one of us is to ask, "What can I do with the talents and abilities that I have?" And you are going to win if you have a greater motivation and capacity for hard work, rather than the person who does not.

Participant: Thank you, Mr Lim. I have a million-dollar question for you, and it has to do with the SMRT. During lunch earlier, I had the privilege of chatting with the engineers at my office, on how to fix the public transport system. They had a whole list of solutions, which I will not elaborate here; the Land Transport Authority probably has better solutions.[2]

But the engineers I spoke to figured that it is more than just an engineering problem; it is probably a policy problem as well. So my question to you is, how do we build a transport system that is SG100-ready? And, how can we do so in a gracious way, in an ungracious society?

---

[2] On 7 October 2017, train services along the North-South Line were disrupted due to a flooding incident and a fire that occurred separately. A quarter of a million commuters were affected by the disruption.

LSG: I am sorry, I left my engineering education behind more than 50 years ago. So, for engineering solutions, I would have to leave it to the technical people.

You had a group of engineers who discussed the issue and had various ideas; the critical question is, "How can they get their ideas through?" It is not necessarily that every idea they put through has to be taken up. But the question is, "How can they get their ideas through so that the people who are in charge would seriously think about them, and see what they can learn from them?" I would say it seems to me that you and your colleagues are already trying to get your ideas through, but you want to be assured that the ideas are seriously considered even if they may not subsequently be taken up for good reason.

When we increasingly become a society where we all have our concerns for the nation, what we want are citizens who ask, "How can we contribute towards making life better?" and "How can we contribute towards making the country stronger?" We have to bear in mind that while we each would have our own views, our views all sit within a whole system and the business of government is really a complex one of deciding a particular course of action from the multiplicity of ideas.

And even though our particular ideas may not be taken up, I think what is most important is for us to be assured that our efforts at putting through our ideas, in our desire to improve things, has been given proper attention. To me, our attitude should be that, as a government and as a people, we should learn from everything and everywhere. Citizens ought to be more willing to offer their views. But not so much on the basis of, "See, I am the smart guy who offered my view; if not for me, the government would not know what to do," but more in terms of, "This is an effort everyone should play their part in."

If we can focus on ideas on how to improve things, it would be good; we put them forward, keep making noise until we are satisfied that people have looked through it and thought about it, banging desks and knocking doors until we get a reasonable explanation as to why our ideas are not taken up. The starting point is to have those ideas in the first place, so I am really very glad to hear about your group of engineers who are keen to do something about the SMRT issue.

KSY: We have a few questions from the rooms outside; I will give you two that are quite related. The first says, "In 2013, Kindness Mascot Singa quit, stating that he was too tired to continue facing an increasingly angry and disagreeable society. What does this say about the state of graciousness in Singapore?" The second question asks, "What is holding us back from being gracious and what can we do to overcome these hurdles?"

LSG: Well, you may consider my answer too simplistic, but it is that we need a cultural change. In my view, we are talking of a change that will take the time of a generation. Therefore, if you start on this journey, I think it will take us 30 years, maybe 40 years, though I hope it takes us much less time. What is critical is that we start.

I pointed out that the way parents do things would affect their children. Well, it would be nice if I can expect that parents would change the whole way in which they bring up their children. But I would also directly address the Gen Ys and the upcoming Gen Zs with this challenge: "If you believe a Gracious Society is what we need and we want, then let us practise it. Practise it in the way that we treat one another in daily life."

These would be little things. For example, when I walk to the office, if I know there are people behind me, I would hold the door open. But do you know how few people say "Thank you"? That does not matter to me, it is the little good I am able to do. I take shuttle buses ever so often — have you ever noticed how many people actually say "Thank you" to the bus driver? These are things that we can practise.

What I am saying to all the young people is that, in many ways, our hopes are with you. Of course, the schools do work very hard at teaching good manners and so forth to the kids. But we should hope very hard that when they go home, their grandparents or parents do not teach them differently. This requires a whole national effort to recognise that many of us are waiting for somebody else to start before we do.

The challenge, then, is for all of us to say, if we believe in this enough, let us start doing it and be the gracious person, rather than look at it in terms of, "This is a tit-for-tat thing, so I will wait for the 'tat' to come first." We should do what we can and maybe in 30 years, we will see a big difference.

I do think that this is a generational change and, therefore, that this is something we cannot wait for the fourth generation to figure out for themselves. Because, even if they figure it out at SG100 that this is what they want to do, they will have to wait for SG150 to see the full results. If we are looking out for SG100, we have to start doing it now.

For those of us who are here, how do you prepare the way so that people will not feel awkward about behaving well? We have a funny situation — some people feel awkward about behaving well because their friends do not like to be shown up. We need to create a whole culture in Singapore where people feel awkward about *not* behaving well.

Participant: I thank Mr Lim for speaking up for the "invisible people", people with disabilities, including invisible ones. Too often, we have people officially in charge of this sector, not being totally aware of how to handle these people. For example, official websites talk about how we can relate to people with autism when they throw tantrums. They are not tantrums; they are meltdowns. We have people in high official circles who do not know what Asperger's Syndrome is, calling it "Asparagus Problem", making fun of the term.

This is not acceptable, and I would like to thank Mr Lim for speaking up on behalf of early childhood needs. Young people with special needs need early intervention programmes. We need to strengthen them. Right now, children with special needs are still left out of the fold of compulsory education, even though we are a signatory to the UN Convention on the Rights of Persons with Disabilities. So I think it is high time we reviewed again this issue of compulsory education for them, and provide more places or resources for people with different abilities, and to embrace people with disabilities.

LSG: If I could make just two points in response to that. First, very often, when you say "the government should do more of this" and "the government should do more of that", there are in fact a million things that people wish for the government to do more of. As I said, the role of government is really to maintain law and order, to provide for the community where the community cannot provide for itself.

At the end of the day, government simply reflects the culture and views of society. This is why, while you can say the government should do more of this or that, at the end of the day, the government is trying to reflect the best way by which they can serve the needs and wishes of society. If society as a whole wants everyone to be looked upon in terms of their strengths and abilities, the government is also going to find itself thinking like that, simply because it is the job of government to reflect the way the society sets its priorities.

I am not saying that government should not do more. All I am saying is that the way the government behaves is to do the best that they can to serve the needs and hopes and wishes of people. Therefore, we have to try to influence the way the whole society thinks. Your point about going out to educate the people so that they know better, is a very good one.

As for how we can deal with people with disabilities, our language should not be one of rights, but one of "How are we doing as a Gracious Society? How are we as human beings, and what does it mean to be doing what is good and what is right?" That is the point I am making. It is not a fight about who shouts loudest or who has bigger rights. It is really about the way society thinks about these things and the values that we hold as a society.

I know that this is not the kind of thing that governments on their own naturally think of. Just like many of us in the way that we run organisations, we like to have KPIs, very specific targets and so forth. What I am advocating here is culture; it is soft transformation. Which is why the issue comes down to whether we all really feel this is important, and whether we believe that it will take us a generation. If so, we must start now. If it takes us just five years, we can still defer it for another five years. It is our own internal convictions that have to move first.

KSY: We are also taking some questions from Facebook and I have three questions here, which are sort of linked. "So, to get to a Gracious Society, can we look at why we even became an ungracious one?", "Do current public policies inhibit gracious behaviour?" and, "Is graciousness compatible with the side effects of meritocracy and competitiveness?"

LSG: Okay, on the first point, how did we come to be like that? My own thesis tends to be that urbanisation makes people like that. We are not unique in Singapore. I think all over the world, you find exactly the same issues. In fact, I have just been reading a book written by the founder of

Kyocera, a well-known Japanese company. The remarkable thing is that he laments about Japanese society, that people there are getting more selfish and less gracious!

So this is by no means unique to Singapore. If we can, in fact, achieve something like a Gracious Society as part of our culture, it will make Singapore truly different from other places. It is not an easy thing to bring about. Urbanisation has, in many ways, created a lot of drive for people to look after themselves, and in a market economy, it is about competition and so forth.

We can look at all these reasons, but then we have to come back to ask, what is important for each one of us, and what can we do about it? In the book written by the founder of Kyocera, he said that, if we have time to complain, it means we have time to do something about it! Well, you know, we may want to agree or not agree with it. But this is what the challenge is about.

To the question about meritocracy, is graciousness related to meritocracy? To me, this is about what we want as a society, it is about fairness and honesty. Hold the government to good standards by insisting: "The government must act in a way which is fair, and a way which is honest, and a way which exhibits integrity." These are good values and expectations that we ought to have for any government that we vote for, any government that is running Singapore. When you look at meritocracy and say that meritocracy is fundamental, then it is about being as fair as we possibly can in the way we choose people for our appointments.

If meritocracy simply refers to what degree you got in university or what grades you got at the "A" Levels, it would be a totally inadequate view of meritocracy. Meritocracy also has to be related to character and motivation. Dee Hock, who is the founder of Visa International, once said, hire and promote people first on the basis of integrity; second, motivation; third, capacity; fourth, understanding; fifth, knowledge; and sixth, experience. Knowledge and experience can easily be built up if you select people based on the first four qualities.

Think about it. First and foremost, you look at people in terms of integrity. The idea is that, without integrity, motivation is dangerous. Without motivation, capacity is impotent. In other words, you have the potential for doing it, but without motivation, you are wasting your capacity. Then he says, without capacity, understanding is limited; you cannot create new stuff and innovation is going to be limited. You need to have understanding to back up capacity. Without understanding, knowledge is meaningless, and without knowledge, experience is blind. Thus without understanding, knowledge becomes misused or underused, and without knowledge, experience does not expand.

When you talk about meritocracy purely in terms of school results, we only get a very, very limited view of meritocracy. Meritocracy has to take into account integrity and motivation and the capacity of people. Yes, we can be unhappy, and yes, we can question the way meritocracy is applied or executed in particular instances. But I think the principle of meritocracy is as fair as we can possibly be in choosing people to get things done.

Does graciousness clash with meritocracy? Graciousness is about the way we treat one another as human beings, what is right, what is fair, what is good. It should not clash with meritocracy at all. If you say meritocracy is a good way by which we best harness what people are capable of contributing to society, then it should not be a choice between graciousness and meritocracy. If the people who reach high levels get there because of meritocracy, I think a heavier responsibility for graciousness lies upon them.

KSY: There was a last question about whether current public policies inhibit gracious behaviour.

LSG: We need to ask what public policy prevents you from being gracious. It is not as though we have a policy that says, "You are not allowed to say thank you and sorry." I find it difficult to think of a policy that does not allow you to be gracious, or where things are made too difficult for you to be so.

But there is no doubt that sometimes we may be organising things in such a way that people begin to behave in a way which is not fair, right, or gracious to one another. In that case, we better do things differently so that we do not induce people to be ungracious to each other.

I have no doubt that there will be occasions where we organise things in such a way that we give full opportunity to people who are ungracious to demonstrate their ungraciousness. But I cannot think of a policy that disallows you to be gracious. But perhaps you can be more specific.

Participant: I have one observation I want to share and relate it to my question. It is on Kampung Spirit. I had the opportunity to stay in Bukit

Ho Swee, where the triad ran the community. But we felt safe. We left the doors open, knowing that nobody would dare to come into our house and steal anything, because there was this culture of a moral society, and the neighbours looked after one another. There was a lot of respect for each other.

Leading on from the last question, I want to throw a spanner in the works. I know that the government is supposed to facilitate a Gracious Society. Therefore should they not set a standard whereby they would respect the population and the wishes for a Gracious Society? What is preventing the government from being more gracious to its citizens? Thank you.

LSG: It is the same question we have for each one of us here: What prevents us from being gracious to one another? Often, it is simply that we do not think about it. We are just not sensitive to it.

Participant: Could I just interject? I think the government sets the tone in a certain way. So I think that, for the government, while the citizens have their own responsibilities, the government has its own too.

LSG: Yes, I agree. Anyway, you have had the airtime to express your point about the government — I am not the government, so it is good that you had the opportunity. But as I mentioned a bit earlier, my own feeling is that if we make progress on this business of people being gracious to one another, the people who serve in the government and the people who make policy are going to be sensitised to it too.

Participant: My question is, how can we sustain this state of affluence, where we can look at graciousness, while maintaining our competitive edge? We know that without that graciousness and the Kampung Spirit, society cannot survive. How can we balance this paradox?

LSG: You would have to come to my next lecture where I would express my thoughts on how we can maintain our competitive edge! Just a preview of what I want to talk about in my last lecture: If we go for a Gracious Society, it is not simply a matter of, "How can we prevent ourselves from blowing up?" It is a question about, "How can we make life so very special in Singapore?" My thesis is really about how we can limit the decline. As you know, under Glubb's thesis, affluence is a catalyst for social decline.

I propose that a Gracious Society is a way by which we can mitigate that decline, so that we do not go through all the consequences of an age of decadence. What I want to talk about in my last lecture is my thesis on how we can create a new S-Curve. I was recently asked in a newspaper interview, the government has said that one to three per cent is the new normal — do I agree? I said, one to three per cent is the new normal if we continue to do the same thing the same way as in the past.

I believe that we have to think differently about the future. What we need to ask is, "In addition to working on how I can limit the decay or the decline after reaching High Noon, can I also think of a way in which I create a new growth, so that the net effect is actually a growth for the country?" I will present my views, but as I said, that is for the next time!

KSY: Thank you, Mr Lim. It sounds like whatever change we want to see by the fourth generation, we have to move now, but we have to move at the speed of trust. Cultural change is going to take a potentially long, slow, and invisible time, so we should all start now. Thank you for your time this evening.

Lecture III

THE WAY OF HOPE

Setting the Foundations for a First-World Society

In my last lecture entitled "The Fourth Generation", I expressed the hope that that generation would have much to celebrate at SG100, but also said that we cannot simply leave it entirely to them to make the Singapore of their time. Certainly, there are many things that they can and should do for themselves. Each generation must solve its own problems. But some things require the work of a generation or more to bring about. And we must start to work on them now, to be in time for that future. A Gracious Society, an important ideal for the First-World Society Singapore aspires to be, is one such thing. It would be a society that makes Singapore stand out from the rest of the world. It would be one that our Fourth Generation will be proud of, and benefit from, because we moved in our generation to lay the groundwork for them to flourish and prosper 50 years later.

For Singapore to sustain a Gracious Society, we would need to continue to grow, and remain sovereign and independent. Because only by being sovereign and independent can we exercise choice in how we want to run our society, how we want to lead our lives, and how we want to make the future for the generations to come.

A Gracious Society, because of its spirit of other-centeredness, will induce better relationships among people and the different sectors of society. There is scope for the public sector to exercise greater sensitivity towards the people in its communications. Similarly, there can be greater attention to employee engagement in businesses and organisations, better service to customers, and greater instinctive concern for issues like income and socio-economic divides.

I know there are already many initiatives for people to help one another, and be kind to one another. There have been many occasions where people spontaneously reach out to help others in trouble. In times of need or crisis, many Singaporeans have shown that they will extend their heart and hands to others. But what we need is to have graciousness in the day-to-day, as an essential feature of our character as a nation. This is culture, an integral part of our make-up as a people.

The Way of Hope

For Singapore to sustain a Gracious Society, we would need to continue to grow, and remain sovereign and independent. Because only by being sovereign and independent can we exercise choice in how we want to run our society, how we want to lead our lives, and how we want to make the future for the generations to come. We would need the continuing capacity to defend ourselves, and we need to be able to earn our keep. We do this by honouring ourselves, our talents, and by honouring our loved ones, neighbours, society, country, and beyond — by giving our best in whatever we do.

This is the focus of my lecture this evening: in the context of building a sustainable Gracious Society, how should we think of our economic development and progress? How do we create hope for ourselves today — and, even more so, for the coming generations? I title my lecture today "The Way of Hope". And if we continue as we are, without changing, I can only call our course, "The Way of Missed Hope".

To get to the future we desire, we need to have grit and resilience to stay the course. But have you not heard this before, in the newspapers and on television? Am I saying anything new?

Our citizens and students in schools are not short on advice. Sometimes, it is for them to have grit and resilience; most recently, it is new skills, innovation and entrepreneurship. But to what purpose? For future jobs and personal success? That is important, but no one can guarantee that!

How do we inspire and unite our people towards this new path, for a cause greater than ourselves? We need to have the imagination to think differently, and the spirit and energy to make the change.

The Gazelle and the Lion

There is an old African saying that goes, "Every day the gazelle wakes up knowing that, if it cannot outrun the fastest lion, it is going to be somebody's breakfast. Every day the lion wakes up knowing that if it cannot outrun the slowest gazelle, it will go hungry."

We may wonder, when we think of Singapore, whether we should see ourselves as the lion or the gazelle.

The first thing to observe is that, whether we are the lion or the gazelle, every day when we wake up, we had better be running. Secondly, while we, as Singaporeans of the Lion City, might naturally think we should be like the lion, it happens to be the wrong answer this time.

There is a big difference whether we run as Number One or Number Two. The lion in the African saying, as Number Two, needs only to follow whatever way the gazelle goes, so long as it keeps up its alertness and its stamina. The gazelle, as Number One, needs not only to run fast, but has to continually assess whether there is a route it can take which the lion cannot follow. So while physical stamina is critical for both lion and gazelle, mental agility is especially critical for the gazelle. I believe Singapore is unique in the world in our geography and our demographics. To have a Number Two frame of mind is the way of mediocrity and perhaps even disaster.

Singapore is known for some of our unique handling of wicked problems, arrived at by learning from best practices elsewhere and the pitfalls to avoid, and adapting our solutions to local conditions. In turn, our provision of public housing to the majority of our population, Central Provident Fund, and healthcare system are policies that are often studied by others overseas.

Of course, we have to be both smart and humble to learn from everyone everywhere, but we have to think for ourselves the best way and create our own smart way. **We need to think as a leader and not as a follower.**

Thinking Graphically

Let me set out the line of my thinking by way of a graph, starting with the reference in my first lecture to the essay, *The Fate of Empires*, by Sir John Glubb.

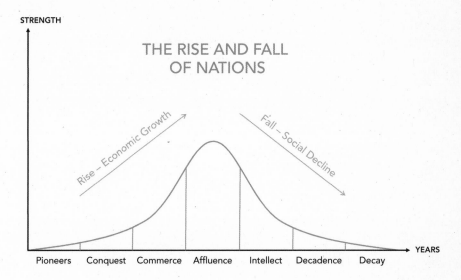

The X-axis represents time, the life of the nation, while the Y-axis represents the strength of the nation. The seven segments represent the seven stages in the rise and fall of nations referred to by Glubb. You start with the Age of Pioneers, then the Age of Conquests, the Age of Commerce, the Age of Affluence, the Age of Intellect, the Age of Decadence, and end with decay. Of course, the Age of Affluence is the time where the nation is at its strongest. What I would like to emphasise here is the Age of Affluence, whereby economic growth is accompanied by complacency and apathy, which in turn catalyse social decay.

In my second lecture, I suggested that, if we could work deliberately at making a Gracious Society the prevailing social culture of Singapore, we could ameliorate the effects of social decay. In graphical terms, this is what I am thinking:

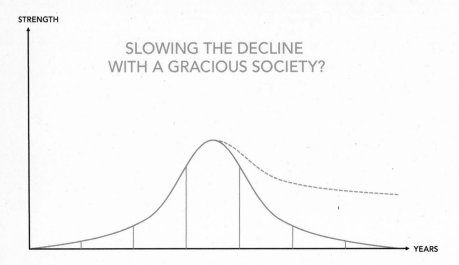

There is the red dashed line where, instead of a fall right down to the bottom, we glide forward more gradually, and we never reach the bottom. The question is: Can we avoid the decline? I do not think we can avoid it altogether, but I believe that we can certainly mitigate the effect if we figure out a way to start a new Age of Pioneers and thereby create a new dimension of Economic Growth. What I mean in graphical terms is the following:

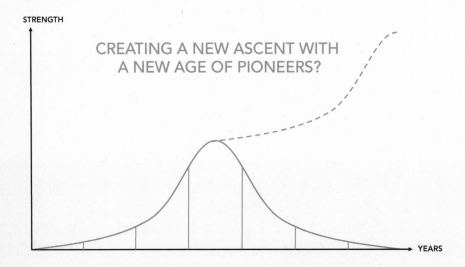

Can we discover a way to start a new S-Curve? What we are doing then, is taking the same curve, and starting again from the Age of the Pioneers. What we are asking ourselves is if there is a way to conceive an Age of New Pioneers? Bear in mind that the pioneers are the ones who break off from the way things are, to create new possibilities, because they conquer new lands and think of new ways of getting things done.

If we were to combine the new ascent with the modified decay — with the idea of a Gracious Society — we end up with the orange dashed line as shown in the following graph:

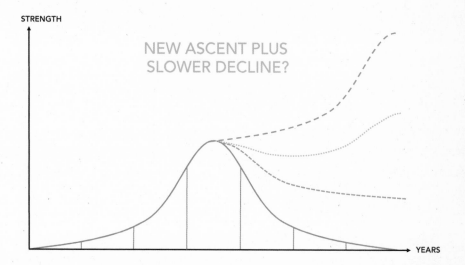

Pursuing this concept, we have to work on bringing about a Gracious Society, which I had presented in the last lecture, in order to diminish the decay. What I would now like to discuss is how we can conceive of the green dotted line so that we end up with the possibility of a new rise. This represents new hope and possibilities for the generations to come. But what will the new ascent be like?

New Age of Pioneers

I had mentioned in my first lecture my belief that Singapore had survived and succeeded in its first 50 years of independence for two reasons. First, by being a people and a government that **Honour Our Word**. We are trustworthy, reliable and dependable. Government policy development is consistent and even predictable. We deliver on our promises, observe the rule of law, and uphold intellectual property rights. We are prepared to learn fast and work hard. Trust is the defining characteristic. Secondly, we **Honour Each Other** as citizens and as human beings. We recognise and appreciate our differences, and make space for each other with respect to race, language, culture and religion. Diversity is the defining characteristic; being a Gracious Society would be an enhanced aspect of this.

Honouring Innovation, Excellence, and Outwardness

But I believe these two aspects of honour, honouring our word and honouring each other, will not be good enough to assure our continuing survival and success. I would like to suggest a third essential aspect of honour for creating a new economic ascent, and it is that we need to be a people who honour innovation, excellence and outwardness. In this aspect of honour, opportunity is the defining characteristic. It has to do with the way we create, identify, develop, and pursue opportunity. Let me explain.

By innovation, I mean any creation, invention, or improvement that has practical value. We need to welcome new ideas and new ways of doing things. We need to think about incremental improvements and step innovations. Someone has remarked, "If you cannot explain how you are innovating, then you are not innovating." I recognise that Singaporeans have been encouraged to innovate for years. But what does it really mean for the ordinary Singaporean when he or she is urged towards "innovation"? Some might perceive it as a technical matter best left to the professionals; some may simply see it as a threat to their "old economy" jobs.

This is a severe cultural challenge for changing values in society, to value best efforts, as opposed to disproportionately rewarding the super A's and gold medals. Nor do we want to simply give everyone a medal for participating.

But what I am talking about is a need for a *culture* of innovation. By culture, I mean for the spirit of innovation to be an integral part of our character and personality as a nation and a society. I do not think we are there now, nor do I think there has been a deliberate and conscious national effort to get to such a cultural transformation.

Let me give you an illustration. Some months back I visited Block 71 at Ayer Rajah. *The Economist* magazine has referred to Block 71 as "the heart of Singapore's technology start-up ecosystem and the world's most tightly packed entrepreneurial ecosystem." It is an exciting place of youthful energy and enthusiasm. During my visit, I asked one of the very excited members of one of the start-ups what was the greatest problem they faced, expecting some technical or business issue they have confronted. Instead, the simple answer I got was, "My mother." This young person had done well in university and could easily have gotten a well-paying job; the mother simply cannot understand why the person is in a start-up, where the rewards are uncertain and even the lifespan of the start-up is uncertain. Parents naturally want their children to be safe and secure.

When I was in Israel recently, I asked, "What do Israeli mothers wish for their children?" The answer I got was, "Twenty years ago, Israeli mothers wished for their children to be doctors or lawyers. Now they wish their children to be CEOs of start-ups." Start-ups and innovation have become an integral part of Israeli culture. We can say the same of Finland and Estonia. Singapore has to get there and be exceptional in our own way.

This requires a cultural and mind-set change, not simply a case of encouraging innovation. As an example of how we need to change our current frame of mind, let me refer to the issue of focusing on high grades and awards. In Singapore, we are inclined to pile accolades on people who have achieved top grades or won gold medals, and leave the others unnoticed and unmentioned. But if we want people to be innovative, which requires them to try more and to learn from failure, we have to recognise people for their effort and not only for their success. Whether or not they have tried their best in exercising their talents and abilities is the critical question, not whether they got the gold medal.

I remember asking a friend whose son had taken part in the Rio Olympics but did not win any medals there, as to what his son was thinking now. He said that his son was seriously considering whether he wanted to spend another four years training and sacrificing other things he could spend his time on.

What would weigh heavily on his son's mind was whether he would be recognised for trying rather than recognised only if he won a medal. Would society think him stupid, or praise his conviction and tenacity? This is a severe cultural challenge for changing values in society, to value best efforts, as opposed to disproportionately rewarding the super A's and gold medals. Nor

An attitude of "satisficing", which means "aiming to achieve only satisfactory results because the satisfactory position is familiar, hassle-free, and secure, whereas aiming for the best achievable result would call for costs, effort, and incurring of risks."

do we want to simply give everyone a medal for participating. There can never be enough airtime and public recognition to go around for every individual. At the same time, there needs to be far more awareness in society on how to notice and nurture the best efforts of others around us.

Excellence

Next, on "Excellence". To me there is only one definition of excellence, which is to be the best we can be. Excellence is not just the next standard in a grading from satisfactory, to good, to very good, and so on. To me, after very good should come "outstanding", rather than "excellent". Excellence, to me, is a measure of performance against potential.

$$\text{EXCELLENCE} \ = \ \frac{\text{PERFORMANCE}}{\text{POTENTIAL}}$$

We have to move away from what appears to be a prevailing attitude on the part of many workers in Singapore — as has been reported in *The Straits Times* — an attitude of "satisficing", which means "aiming to achieve only satisfactory results because the satisfactory position is familiar, hassle-free, and secure, whereas aiming for the best achievable result would call for costs, effort, and incurring of risks."

When we avoid "trying our best", by simply doing what is good enough, we are in fact cheating ourselves of what is possible, given our individual talents and abilities. This is not just something for the government to do, but something that depends very much on the attitude of the individual Singaporean towards work and life. The call often heard for work-life balance is understandable, but regrettable if it is a call to be allowed to *not be* excellent, to *not do* the best possible, and to *not be* the best possible. The government can provide incentive schemes and the infrastructure, but it cannot supply the passion and conviction.

I was speaking to someone who said he had heard so much about the start-up environment in Singapore, so he decided to go for a drive around Block 71 on a Saturday night. He found the whole place dark, something he would never find in Ho Chi Minh City in Vietnam. I quote this not to fault the Singaporeans, but for Singaporeans to realise others are not like us.

Outwardness

Finally, about "Outwardness". Some years back, I was in Shanghai and decided to take the opportunity to speak with CEOs of Singapore companies that had substantial operations in China. One of them was planning to expand his network of stores in China. I said that would be a wonderful opportunity for Singapore students to get internship opportunities for exposure in China. This CEO replied that he would be prepared to take many of such students, but, "You know," he added, "they tell me 'Beijing okay, Shanghai okay, Xi'an not okay.'" In other words, Singaporeans want to go where things are familiar and predictable. They are not adventurous to try new things and work with the unfamiliar and the uncomfortable. They are not curious to confront what they do not know and to learn from every situation.

> The call often heard for work-life balance is understandable, but regrettable if it is a call to be allowed to *not be* excellent, to *not do* the best possible, and to *not be* the best possible. The government can provide incentive schemes and the infrastructure, but it cannot supply the passion and conviction.

This is a serious problem. Often, when I am asked what is my best advice for young people looking for their first job, I say, "Chase the opportunities, don't chase the money." Money is what you get for what you already know and what you already can do. Opportunities are what allow you to build your future with expanded knowledge and experience. "Don't chase the money; let the money chase you."

Another point about Outwardness. No foreign investor brought to Singapore by the Economic Development Board (EDB) is in Singapore *for* the Singapore economy. They are all here to use Singapore as the base to reach out into the region or globally. Singapore companies that want to grow and expand should similarly position themselves well to go into the region and the world. By all means, use Singapore as the test bed for new ideas, but the end goal cannot be Singapore.

The world's largest economies by 2050 are likely to be China, India, the United States, and ASEAN, in descending order. In other words, three of the four largest economies will be in Asia, with Singapore more or less geographically at the centre of them. It would be silly of us not to recognise the opportunity this represents, especially as we also note our major racial composition to be Chinese, Malay and Indian. But this opportunity can only yield value if Singaporeans are outwardly oriented, not inwardly focused.

I quote you yet another example. There was someone who had worked with me in the Civil Service many years ago who one day decided to leave for another career that involved working in a variety of other countries. After 10 years, the officer decided to return to Singapore. The officer found a job with a well-established firm, but wondered why the firm needed to have so many expatriates in senior positions. After a year, the officer remarked, "All the expats are required." If the firm had a new business opportunity in an unfamiliar part of the world, the expatriate was more than likely to say, "When do you want me to go?" The Singaporean, on the other hand, is more likely to say, "Let me consult my wife," who, after consulting Google Search, is more than likely to say, "Too dangerous — don't go."

Please do not get me wrong. It is good to consult our spouse and to think about the needs of our family, always. There is nothing wrong with the Singaporean's decision to not go, and to prefer instead the security and comfort of Singapore, but the Singaporean must then be prepared to accept that his economic value to the firm is not as high as that of the expatriate.

Trust, Diversity, and Opportunity

My formula for Singapore to be able to start a new age of pioneers and make a new economic ascent that breaks away from the past is to go beyond "honour our word" and "honour each other" to "honour innovation, excellence and outwardness"; I can summarise these three legs of honour as Honour Trust, Honour Diversity, and Honour Opportunity.

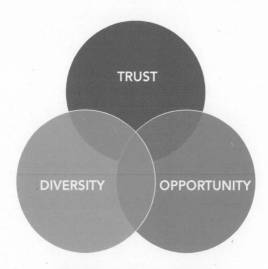

THREE LEGS OF HONOUR

But to get value out of this, we have to understand it as a matter of culture — the way we think and act and live as Singapore and Singaporeans. Because culture takes a long time to shape or reshape, it is an inter-generational challenge that needs leadership and consistency of effort, behaviour and action now.

The Power of Culture — Values Lived Out

Professor Rosabeth Moss Kanter of Harvard Business School has pointed out that financial results are a "lagging indicator" of a company's health. "They tell you what you've just done. They don't predict the future. Culture is a leading indicator. Culture predicts the future."[1] She adds that culture is "more important in some ways than strategy," and that "[if] you're not thinking about building your culture for survivability and sustainability, then you're not leading." These are tough words, but nonetheless words of wisdom. I believe that what Kanter says of business applies just as much to nations. Gross Domestic Product and employment figures are a lagging indicator. National culture predicts the course of progress and development of countries.

Bearing in mind that culture refers to the collection of values that are lived out in the thinking and behaviour of the people in a company or country, let us now listen to Mr Jack Ma, Founder and Chairman of Alibaba Group, who spoke of the power of values in a message to the Honour International Symposium 2016.[2]

I believe mutual trust and credibility is the biggest undiscovered fortune
那我相信，信任、互信是最大的未开发财富

Still from Jack Ma's message to the Honour International Symposium 2016.

Some time ago, I was asked what I meant by "honour". As you see, Jack Ma himself said that "honour" is such a difficult word, and he had

---

[1] HBS Working Knowledge, "Why Uber Is Worth Saving, And How To Save It," *Forbes*, 30 June 2017. Accessed 29 November 2017. Retrieved from: https://www.forbes.com/sites/hbsworkingknowledge/2017/06/30/why-uber-is-worth-saving-and-how-to-save-it/#e92e8d3449f0.

[2] Watch the video here: https://www.youtube.com/watch?v=n1s8I2xREZs

a difficult time trying to identify the Chinese character that conveys the point. My answer is that we need to understand the deeper meaning of "honour". To discover this deeper meaning, we should ask ourselves, what is the difference between "liking" and "loving"? We know very often that people use the word "love" as meaning "like a lot", but that is the kind of degradation in the use of words that results in the loss of their deeper meaning. If you say you like someone or something, it means there is some feature in that thing or some characteristic of that person which appeals to you. "Liking" is actually thinking about yourself. On the other hand, to say that you love someone, you will be continually asking, "What can I do to make the other person more comfortable? What can I do to make the other person happier?"

So, "loving" is really thinking about the other person. This is the same idea behind honour. If you say you honour someone, you are thinking about the other person rather than thinking of yourself. This is what the idea of building a Gracious Society is about. The fundamental idea behind a Gracious Society is thinking about others, and treating them as fellow Singaporeans, as human beings. A Gracious Society is about "other-centredness".

Lessons from Finland and the Grameen Bank

Let me go on to speak a little bit more about this culture of innovation, excellence and outwardness, because this is what I believe Singapore needs to build up for an Age of New Pioneers. One might assert that culture needs to evolve on its own, but I am afraid we do not have the time for natural evolution, because technology and the world are moving too fast.

Modern Singapore was never a product of pure chance or "natural evolution". And we are not alone. Finland, for example, recently carried out a total revamp of its education system to build it around a firm belief in entrepreneurship as the future for Finland. Students are taught skills for entrepreneurship. These skills are not just "hard technical skills", which tend to be how skills are often narrowly understood in Singapore. Rather, these skills also involve a heavy dose of "soft skills" which include leadership, project management, and the ability to work as a team. I am told that a project for students equivalent to what would be Primary Six in Singapore could be to set up a bank!

He told me that he was going around schools in Israel to set up robotics clubs. I know many schools in Singapore have robotics clubs too. I asked him what they did in his clubs. He said all the members had to go through lessons in social responsibility.

Finland today probably has the highest number per capita of what are termed "unicorns" — start-ups worth more than USD1 billion each. Despite having a population slightly smaller than Singapore's, it has its sights on producing four Nokias, the hugely successful cell phone company that had unfortunately missed the turning on smart phones, but is seeing a resurrection of its fortunes with new technological developments. Finland is also the home of the very popular mobile game "Angry Birds". These successes have allowed the Finns to look at the target of four Nokias as believably achievable. Singapore must find our own way to promote a *culture* of innovation so that it is the way of life for us — what we are — and not just something we do.

I recently had the opportunity to hear Professor Muhammad Yunus, the Bangladeshi social entrepreneur, banker, economist and civil society leader who was awarded the Nobel Peace Prize in 2006 for founding the Grameen Bank and pioneering the concepts of microcredit and microfinance. He said every human being has two parts: the selfish part and the selfless part. The world tends to keep feeding the selfish part. The fundamental reason why the Grameen Bank has succeeded when the great majority of institutions who have tried microcredit and microfinance have failed is that the philosophical foundation of Grameen Bank is on feeding the selfless part of the human being.

Professor Yunus observed that the great majority of Grameen Bank loans had gone to women. A critical way in which those women who had succeeded through the Grameen Bank loans had spent their newfound income was to provide their children with a good education. Professor Yunus then heard that after completing their formal education, a good number of these children had lamented that they could not find jobs. On hearing this, he told them to stop complaining about not having jobs, but instead to set up their own businesses. The children responded that they did not know how to do so. He told them to go and learn from their mother. This is entrepreneurship in real life: people who have to do things for themselves and imagine possibilities for themselves, rather than wait for somebody to create jobs and work for them.

Values and Soft Skills

Let me quote another example of how critical values and "soft skills" are. I have a friend in Israel who is now retired. When I met him recently, he told me that he was going around schools in Israel to set up robotics clubs. I know many schools in Singapore have robotics clubs too. I asked him what they did in his clubs.

Academic results are simply not good enough. Being trustworthy and willing to think, try, learn, lead and serve are possibly even more important. To deal with a future that is uncertain and changes quickly, we need to realise that the relevance of particular hard skills may well be limited to a few years, while that of most soft skills are likely to be beneficial for a generation at least.

He said all the members had to go through lessons in social responsibility. I would never have expected such a need for members of robotics clubs. He explained that robots have to benefit society, so members of robotics clubs need to be trained to think about benefits to society. He added that another lesson members of robotics clubs had to learn was how to cope with failure. The robotics club members were all aiming to take part in international robotics competitions. Most of them would never win, so it is essential that the students learn how to cope with failure.

If Singapore hopes to be a nation of enterprise and innovation, we need to do likewise in emphasising values and "soft skills" in our schools, and higher education and continuous learning in society. But we need to recognise that values and soft skills cannot be taught the same way as hard skills. They have to be demonstrated, practised, and absorbed in daily life, not just by children and students, but by community leaders, public servants, employers, parents, adults — everyone. Academic results are simply not good enough. Being trustworthy and willing to think, try, learn, lead and serve are possibly even more important. To deal with a future that is uncertain and changes quickly, we need to realise that the relevance of particular hard skills may well be limited to a few years, while that of most soft skills are likely to be beneficial for a generation at least.

Reaching Out to Singapore's Potential

Singapore needs to succeed ahead of other nations *not* as a matter of pride or ambition, but as a simple matter of surviving despite the odds against us. What a country can become really depends on just three factors, namely, geography, demographics and technology. Technology can make up for — but only to some extent — the physical limitations of geography. Similarly, technology can make up for — again, only to some extent — the human limitations of demographics. What technology cannot do is to substitute for smart immigration, productive work attitudes, and efforts to maximise the development of human talents and abilities.

Well-conceived economic policy can produce the greatest benefit from an optimal mix of geography, demographics and technology. But how much of such economic policy may actually be implemented depends on how much room there is to do so within the realm of domestic politics. The degree of openness and sense of urgency of Singaporeans to such change will decide how much of the good ideas may be adopted. It is a supportive combination of political culture, innovation culture, excellence culture, outwardness culture and change culture that will make the future for Singapore.

Singaporeans need a strong sense of self-confidence and courage that comes from much trying and learning from doing. However, self-confidence and courage cannot be built up by talking or through lectures, but by active learning, and failing, and improving, and trying again. Will parents allow schools to give assignments where answers are not clear, results are not certain, and which their children will not only find difficult, but may actually fail to get to the final targets?

I was speaking to a school principal recently where she lamented that her school organised trips for their students to spend time in a kampung in Malaysia for the experience of a new environment to help develop enterprise and self-confidence. Many parents had refused to grant approval for their children to go. She asked me how I would deal with such a situation. I said, I would meet all these parents and tell them that the ever-evolving and uncertain future would require their children to be able to cope with new experiences and unfamiliar situations. By not allowing their children to go, they are actually denying their children new opportunities to gain self-confidence and courage, which can only be developed by living through the experience. They would be disadvantaging their children as compared to those who were going.

Confidence in Overcoming Our Limitations

I have now spoken over three lectures on the theme, "Can Singapore Fall?" Of course Singapore can fall. But we can choose to organise ourselves so that we have little reason to fall. I once met a Swiss professor who is familiar with our universities in Singapore. I asked him — as Singaporeans so often do when we meet expatriates and foreigners — what we can do better. He responded, "That is the problem with you Singaporeans. You are very capable in many fields. But you don't know it or do not accept it; you don't build upon what you already are capable of to produce new ideas and try new ways." I take the professor's words to heart. If we think we can, we can!

The geographical limitations we face will always be with us, and climate change will no doubt pose new challenges. But if we choose to confront these adversities directly, take confidence in what we already have and know, learn from everywhere but think for ourselves, refuse to be put down by others or to put ourselves down, choose action over talking, and move with purpose and urgency, I am confident that we will surprise even ourselves.

Winning as Both City and State

Singapore is both city and state, so winning a good future for ourselves must mean winning both as city and as a state. While one to three per cent economic growth may be the new normal for developed economies of nation states larger than us, it is highly questionable as an acceptable new normal for us as a city when other cities are growing at a significantly faster pace. How can Singapore be satisfied with one to three per cent when cities in the region and elsewhere could be growing much faster? Jakarta is probably growing at a rate of something like 10 per cent, for example.

Higher economic growth will give us greater options in dealing especially with the social challenges coming upon us particularly from a rapidly ageing population — indeed Singapore has been identified as a super-ageing society — and a diminishing indigenous workforce. To get higher growth rates requires higher productivity — which we can get through a drive for innovation, excellence, and outwardness — but also a larger workforce, if we are prepared to recognise our need for it.

When I was Chairman of the EDB, I met the CEO of a large global company that had set up a significant research centre in Singapore. However, it had also recently set up a substantially larger research centre in Shanghai in the same field. So I posed the question point-blank to him as to whether he was going to close down the Singapore centre in favour of the Shanghai centre. His response was highly instructive. He said, "We go to wherever the talent is."

What this means is that if Singapore does not seek to attract and take in whatever beneficial capability and people that are available from outside Singapore, in addition to developing the talents and abilities of Singaporeans, enhanced economic activity will not happen, and our signal to the world will simply be, "It is okay." But is it *really* okay?

Of course, we must always insist that when a Singaporean is most capable of taking on a job, the job must go to them and not to a non-Singaporean. This is meritocracy at work. Meritocracy is the smartest way by which a small nation like Singapore can make its future from the human capital available to us.

The smallness of Singapore should also be used to our advantage in terms of speed and experimentation, but it must be experimentation with a view to scaling up for the world outside Singapore. Technology is a matter of life and death for us, as it must be for all small nations, so every Singaporean student must know technology. At the same time, graciousness is what will make Singapore a great place to live in, and give meaning and purpose to the eternal striving for survival that is Singapore's destiny. Being a Gracious Society would unlock what David Halpern has referred to as "the hidden wealth of nations", where the extent to which citizens get along with others independently drives both economic growth and well-being.

Much of what we can become depends on us, the citizens. It is a choice of whether to "die" in due time, on account of complacency and apathy, or to live well because we act in good time to do the things which will take a long time to establish. Culture takes time to shape, but culture also becomes the foundation of strength that cannot be easily broken. What we need most of all is not maps — no one else is in our position, and no one else's map will get us to where our strengths can get us to. We have to move forward with our own compass of values, to honour our word, honour each other, honour innovation, excellence and outwardness.

The Honour Circle

I close with what I call the Honour Circle: start with honour-driven individuals, who will do all they can with their talents and abilities. This builds up honour-driven families, where children grow in self-confidence and strong values, which they imitate from, and practise with, their parents and siblings. We then go to honour-driven communities, of which a Gracious Society is a key feature. Next, we have honour-driven organisations, which may be businesses or civic organisations, where superior leadership allows people to be the best they can be and do the best they can in pursuit of innovation, excellence and outwardness. Finally, we have the honour-driven nation, where culture and values and clear leadership in government and our national institutions create the foundation for honour-driven individuals to thrive and be the best they can be.

THE HONOUR CIRCLE

Singapore Need Not Fall

In summary, we can look forward to a thriving, successful Singapore if we:

- Maintain our nation brand value of integrity and trustworthiness
- Use our diversity in race, language, culture and religion for synergistic effect
- Have facility with technology and continuous change

- Focus on identifying, developing and harnessing talents and abilities at all levels
- Release the energy and imagination of the young to be involved in national life
- Take advantage of the rise of Asia, the Internet and the middle class
- Urgently establish a culture of innovation, excellence and outwardness

Thank you, and my very best wishes for a future whose potential we must try to see clearly, choose deliberately, and build now, so that our grandchildren and great grandchildren can still call Singapore home, where they have the best chances for being the best they can be!

Question-and-Answer Session
Moderated by Dr Gillian Koh

Gillian Koh (GK): It is a great privilege to be chairing this session. Mr Lim was the former Head of Civil Service, former Chairman of EDB, and I think a good part of the public sector refer to him as "Yoda".

Mr Lim, you depicted your Honour Circle with five categories, but throughout your lecture, I was anticipating five concentric circles, with the family — comprising individuals, of course — at the heart of it. You described someone in Block 71 saying that the key hurdle he faced in what he was doing was his mother. You described a principal saying that the key hurdle she faced in developing the soft skills that our next generation will need was the parents. So it sounded to me that, at the heart of it, should be the family and individuals.

But since you set them out on an equal plane, let me pose the political question: Parents will then say in response, "No! It is the education system and the educators that are the reason for us becoming a more risk-averse society, the hurdle for my children to be doing something different."

How do we unlock this? You spoke about having a politics of openness. We are in this phase of our national life where we are trying to take ground views. You talked about this conundrum, so how do we crack it — be it the struggle of parents over their children's education, the means to obtain a new

S-Curve of innovation, or other conundrums that we will face, to achieve the way of hope?

Lim Siong Guan (LSG): The reason for not having concentric circles with the family right in the centre is that this gives the impression that all you need to do is fix the family, and everything else will be fixed. I do not think so. The family does its bit, and then when their child goes to school, what does the child face? The parent may say, "Be adventurous, try new things", but the teacher says, "Be safe, otherwise I get into trouble." On the other hand, if the school says, "Be adventurous, try new things", the parents may say, "I do not want my children to be exposed to these dangers." So that is a problem.

Later, when the child enters work, what does he face? If he discovers that there is no point taking risks — because all the smart people who do not take risks get promoted, whereas when he does take risks and fails, he gets condemned — he ends up not trying new things.

This is why my belief is that honour has to go around in a circle because every part of society needs to believe in it, to say, "We better do this, otherwise we are all dead."

There is no doubt that everything starts with the parents. The Chinese have a saying, "By the time the child is three years old you can see how the child is going to be like when he is grown up." I have a Japanese friend, and I asked him if the Japanese have such a saying, and he said they do. The Jesuits say, "Give me a child till seven and I will give you the man." Then I asked an Indian friend who said that the Indians are somewhere in between: "The Tamils have a saying that by five years old, you can tell how a child is going to be like!"

Anyway, everybody agrees that by the time the child turns up in school, his attitude towards life and work is mostly settled — how much curiosity he has, and whether he learns to be adventurous. That is not to say schools cannot mould the child in a different way, but a lot starts from home. If the parents disallow something, it will not happen, because the teachers will listen to the parents; they will not take the risk of doing otherwise. So, everyone needs to do their part, but we must first believe that we need to be different from what we are now, if we are going to be different in our future.

GK: To make these big policy shifts, which comes first — do people make the change and then the government follows, or does the government make the changes decisively, then the people follow?

LSG: I think we have a situation today where we face a new generation — let us say, the Gen-X, then Gen-Y, then Gen-Z coming through, where people feel that they want to make up their mind for themselves. Indeed, if the government were to take the initiative for many of these things, the moment the government opens its mouth, people will say, "That is all propaganda" or "That is all self-serving", so they are not going to listen.

We face a very serious problem. It is not unique to Singapore; it is like that all over the world. What makes it particularly serious for Singapore is that we are a small place. But this also offers us a much greater opportunity to jump in front and build ourselves up. At the same time, we are not any different in terms of what our young people expect.

As a general point, the government, led by the People's Action Party, has said for a long time that they do not believe in a politics of expedience. This means that they do not do things simply because it is popular or comfortable, but are prepared to do things that are very important for our survival and success for generations to come. So, instead of having a politics of expedience, they say, "Let us have a politics of explanation," meaning that they have to do tough things but will explain to the people who voted the government in as to why those tough things are necessary.

I think, though, we need to recognise that the level of intrinsic trust has been somewhat diminished — not necessarily because of what the government in Singapore has done, but as a general trend all over the world. It is not a case of there being no trust at all. It is a case of, "We would like very much to be able to trust the government," but the government cannot simply say, "This is my explanation."

I think the challenge for the future is to move to a politics of conviction; politics in Singapore has to move to one where the government needs to recognise that it has to convince Singaporeans on the need for policy change. They have now to say, "I cannot assume that you will trust me so that all I need to do is to explain to you what I propose to do." Now, the government has to go a step further, to say, "I need to communicate well; I need to demonstrate the necessity for change; I need to be able to convince you."

Indeed, I do not believe that, today, even a politics of conviction is good enough for Singapore. I think we need to move on to what I call a politics of *involvement* — in other words, a politics that requires people themselves to be involved in the process of thinking and doing.

I mentioned in my second lecture that the difficulty about creating a Gracious Society is that the government cannot deliver it, because it is about the quality of the relationship between citizens. It is something that the individual citizen has to bring about. The government may facilitate or encourage it, but they cannot bring it about. Therefore, the challenge for Singapore is not just a politics of conviction, where the government focuses on communication and leadership in order to convince the population of what is good for Singapore's future. It is to go on to a politics of involvement, which says, "We need to involve people in the process because people want to feel that they are shaping the future, or at least they have a major part in influencing the future and shaping the future." This is a lot tougher.

GK: And now it is time to involve the audience in this event.

Participant: As what Mr Lim said, the people need to play their part, but little is mentioned about what the government needs to do to play their part. Why is it that our innovation and technology companies such as Razer do not even do their IPO in Singapore, going to Hong Kong or China instead? Even when Razer built the Razer mobile phone, they do not sell it in Singapore!

Government officials need to ask why our innovative Singaporeans are not basing themselves in Singapore. Why does Joseph Schooling have to go to the US to train? Why does Mixed Martial Arts fighter Angela Lee have to go to the US? Do we have the space here for them to be innovative?

LSG: This is why we cannot simply have concentric circles — everybody must play their part in a Gracious Society. Frankly, in the case of Joseph Schooling, he needed to be performing at world standards to get his gold medal, and therefore needed to compete against other people who are of that standard. If he had not, he would never have pushed himself far enough. If you do not compete against people of that standard, you will never be able to discover the limits of what you are capable of doing. In his case, Joseph Schooling went to the US to our advantage, so what is the problem with that?

We have no problem going anywhere in the world to make use of opportunities to learn, get experience, and so forth. Similarly, for Razer, their primary and largest market is actually the US. I do not believe that they did not want to list in Singapore or sell Razer phones in Singapore. It was purely a case of cost analysis; everything runs by economics. Razer, being a business, has to think in terms of costs, about where it makes the most economical sense to get things done.

If we say that Singapore businesses must be confined to just Singapore, that way of thinking will kill our businesses. Instead, our businesses must say, "Where in the world can I go and take advantage of all the possibilities?" The reality is, Razer has quite a considerable research and development headquarters in Singapore, to build up ideas and designs for their products, although they have another headquarters in San Francisco because their primary market is there.

The important thing for our companies is to be clear in their minds that Singapore may represent an opportunity as a test-bed to start and build up, but Singapore cannot be their end goal. The Singapore market is too small for them to be able to realise their full potential.

Participant: In the earlier part of the lecture, you talked about how the fourth generation should create a Gracious Society. Does that mean creating a nation that Singaporeans will be proud of, or is it essential to Singapore's future survival and success?

LSG: I think Gracious Society contributes towards Singapore's future, as well as the nature of Singapore's society. I take this idea of a Gracious Society from the book by David Halpern about the *Hidden Wealth of Nations*. He says that the hidden wealth of nations is in fact the quality of the relationships among the citizens. The quality of the relationship is not simply a matter of, "Life is okay in terms of the way people treat each other"; it has a direct impact on economic growth.

Fundamentally, the idea is about creating a society where there is good social grease all around, and there are people who respect one another as human beings and think about others. I am also sure that a Gracious Society will lead to the civil service always thinking about the businesses and the people it is serving. This will help to bring about a situation where leaders in government and companies are going to think more naturally about the effect of policies and practices on their employees, customers, and the public they are dealing with.

The idea of a Gracious Society is a perspective that says, "There is something integral to our being, whereby we always think of the other person and the effect upon them of what we do." This will be a powerful factor in the success of businesses, of government itself, and of us as a society.

Participant: Good evening, Mr Lim. Throughout the lecture, you talked about the need to build a Gracious Society, to feed the selfless part of the human being. This, in a sense, speaks of a non-zero-sum society. How does this come about, or can this come about when we live in a meritocratic society that is fundamentally zero-sum?

LSG: How does this come about when we live in a meritocratic society? Well, the whole point of my remarks is that we are *not yet* there. I am sharing my thoughts about how we can get there. Before we can say how to get there, we must first have a very good idea about where it is we want to go, and what it is that we want to become. There is no doubt that we would have to work on it.

To your point on a meritocratic society, I know of a school in Singapore where they have this tradition where the top class of each grade occupies classrooms in their central block. That is a badge of honour. Now, in order to get there, there are no individual ranking standards; it is not that they rank students and the first 40 go to the top class, the next 40 go to the next, and so on. Instead, what the school does is to keep the Secondary One class groupings the same, so that the students will continue on with one another into Secondary Two, and so forth.

Now, when you do that, and when the top class is decided on the average of the marks of the whole class, meritocracy is about everybody in the whole class succeeding, not about individuals succeeding. In order to get to the top, you have a situation now where the not-so-bright students want the brightest ones in their class. In fact, they want the brightest students to be as bright as possible! And the bright students want to do what they can to help the not-so-bright students so that they do not pull the class average down. It is a matter of how we organise ourselves and the perspective we take. It is one of, "I want the best possible people with me, because that is the best way by which we can achieve the most. At the same time, I want to do everything I can to help the weaker ones, to raise them up."

The key is for everyone to try to be the best that they can be, and doing the best they can. This is the essence of meritocracy. It is not about predefining who shall go up and who shall not. It is about saying, "How do we create conditions so that everyone can do their best according to their talents and abilities?" And that has to be our definition of meritocracy — it is not about pre-selection.

Participant: I understand from your lecture that there is a need for us to embrace these values and attitudes for the purposes of survival and economic growth. But is this a compromise on our national level of happiness or individual happiness? If you look at other countries — even just at Singaporeans around us — I am not sure if we are a really happy people. If these attitudes and values you speak of are actually founded on economic growth, will it exacerbate the situation, or is this a compromise?

LSG: If you look at the world according to per capita GDP, by some accounts, Qatar is Number One. Singapore's last ranking was around Number Five. Before us, I think you have Luxembourg and Liechtenstein.

I do not think we are going to be any happier even if we become Number One in the world. Therefore, clearly the key of our future — in terms of a better life — does not lie in becoming Number One in terms of GDP per capita. I agree with you on that.

Now, what is happiness? All of you have heard of Maslow's Hierarchy of Needs, which I introduced in my second lecture. If I were to ask people how many needs there are, some people say five, some people say six, some say seven. But when I ask them what the highest need is, everybody can tell me what it is: self-actualisation. Of course, everybody can remember that because it is all about the selfish self! This is the point that Muhammad Yunus was talking about: feeding your selfish side.

The remarkable thing is that later research showed that Maslow's Hierarchy of Needs is inadequate. There are three more needs in addition to the five. The original hierarchy first had your physiological needs, and then your safety needs, then your love needs — because all of us need this sense of being loved by somebody — followed by esteem needs — all of us need this sense of being respected by other people. Then there are our cognitive needs: all of us want to understand what is going on, and why we are being asked to do the things we are asked to do. Then come aesthetic needs: we all need to have a sense of beauty, balance, and order in our lives. And after aesthetic needs comes self-actualisation, the sense that we are now on the best path of being the best that we can be. Self-actualisation is about our potential compared to where we are, right? So, self-actualisation is about being the best that we can be.

But researchers later discovered that the highest need of all is transcendence. Transcendence comes from helping other people become the best that they can be. It is terribly interesting that the highest level of happiness that we can have is to give happiness to other people.

The remarkable thing is the conclusion that the deepest sense of happiness that we all can have as individuals is this sense that we are capable of helping other people. I am sure many of us feel this. This is why people spend time looking after the handicapped and the aged, why people spend time doing community service, why CEOs of companies, having reached the pinnacle of their career, decide that they do not mind spending time working with the people sector.

So, whenever we all think that the best thing for each one of us is self-actualisation, we should just try to take one more step, and ask: what do we get when we help other people be the best that they can be? We get a sense of satisfaction from doing something good for the lives of other people.

Among all the professions, teachers are virtually the only ones who have found the secret to satisfaction. Why do I say that? The really interesting thing about teachers is that they say, "My job is to do the best that I can with each child that comes to me. It is to help each child be the best he or she can possibly be. Therefore, if later in life, this child goes to a higher socio-economic level, I have succeeded. The more this child exceeds me in later life, the more successful I have been." And the satisfaction of the teacher is to feel that they have done what they can to bring the child up to become the best he or she can be.

In all other jobs that we have, too often we do not look at the people under us as a privilege given to us to help each of them be the best that they can be. Instead, we look at them as tools given to us, to serve us and help us get promoted. I think we need to change our perspective to one where we see our peers and the people who work under us as a privilege that is given to us to do some great things for their lives. As I said, the interesting thing is that teachers, in a natural kind of way, are probably the only ones getting this truth in daily work.

GK: Mr Lim, you said in your lecture that we are a small city-state, so we have to find ways to survive; we have to be the gazelle. On the other hand, you also said to the young people, "Do not chase the money. Chase the opportunities and let the money follow." Do you want to say something about how survival is not about chasing the money, but about fulfilling your fullest potential, because then the money will chase you if you have got the great idea?

LSG: The amount of money that chases you depends on what you are capable of. The more you reach the full capacity of your abilities, the more money will chase you.

GK: But Singaporeans need to get to the point where they are fulfilling their greatest potential and the money chases them.

LSG: Oh absolutely! The same principle applies to a country. Very often when I speak to audiences of Singaporeans, they talk about how we should not get foreigners in and should reserve everything for ourselves. I tell them the problem will resolve itself; when Singapore goes down, foreigners will stop wanting to come to Singapore anyway, so do not worry about them!

A better perspective to take on non-Singaporeans will be, "Please join us because if you can help grow the size of our pie, we are happy to have you. You are not coming here for the purpose of just helping us; you come here because it is good for your life." Having everybody work together is the perspective of a team. How do you create a situation where everybody can contribute the best they can? Nevertheless, as I said in my second lecture, if you have a situation of two people being equally capable, you must make sure, as a country, that the Singaporean is chosen. I think that is the fairest thing we can do, and even the non-Singaporean can understand why this is so, because in their own country, that is what they fully expect to be the rule of the game.

Participant: I want to touch a little about this "culture thing" and how it seems to be the essence of the future of Singapore. In my generation, the culture was hard work, self-sacrifice, "do things for the country," etc. We were brought up that way, and I suppose that has contributed to Singapore's success. But we know now that the culture seems to be one of "Me for myself, chase the money, I only get paid if you give me good credit for whatever it is." You can see this clear change and of course, you know the flavour of the month is SMRT, which also has deep cultural problems, according to the CEO![3]

You were Head of Civil Service for a long time. You had a front-row seat in seeing this change happen. Can you give us a kind of inside view on what explains this phenomenon, from a culture of high-mindedness to this culture of, "I will only work if the money is there"? What are some of your insights from the front bench?

Participant: Thank you for your example of teachers who are supposed to be teaching people how to be their best. I have two encounters, which I hope you will take as feedback on how government policy has to change. My grandniece attended one of the top schools here. When the time came for assessments, she had transferred out of Singapore and the teacher was very happy about it. She said, "Well I am glad you are taking your daughter out of my class because her grades are pulling down the grades of the class."

There was another instance where my friend, whose daughter liked mathematics but was an average student, was told by the teacher to take his

---

[3] In his public statement on 16 October 2017, SMRT Group Chief Executive Officer Desmond Kuek attributed the recent train disruptions, which affected hundreds of thousands of commuters, to human error and failure, citing "deep-seated cultural issues" within the company that would require more time than earlier anticipated to root out.

daughter out of her class because the daughter's grades were pulling down the grades of the class as well! To me, it is like, hey, what is happening?

You said it correctly: Everybody has to do their part. But in my experience, what the government does, how they assess teachers can have an impact on the children and ruin our future.

GK: Thank you. So, how does cultural change happen, and what is going on in the education system?

LSG: Let me address the second question first. As you said, they are your observations and feedback. The next time I give such a lecture, you should bring the teachers in to listen to me!

But may I say this: In all fairness, obviously teachers and every one of us are going to react according to the way that we are assessed. If the teacher feels that she is going to be assessed on the basis of grades in class, she will act that way. If she believes that she is going to be assessed on the basis of, for instance, "value add", then that is a different way of assessment.

A few years after I left the Ministry of Education (MOE), McKinsey did a study asking, "What is the best education system in the world?", in order to come to certain conclusions as to how they can be helpful to schools all over the world to improve the quality of the education. This lady in Dubai, who was the lead consultant, called me up and asked, "There's one thing which we found thoroughly curious in Singapore, and that is, you do not pay teachers bonuses according to the results of the class. You do not have that kind of incentives, and yet, Singapore keeps coming up with these really excellent results in the PISA scores. We do not understand that."

You can understand that consultants always would like to have a formula. "This is my formula. If you follow my formula, you get these results." So Singapore is very puzzling to them because we do not have a formula that they can use, and proceed to tell people how to get results. By the way, in the US, where some states had invoked the practice of incentivising teachers according to class results, most of them have reversed their policies. Why so? Because they discovered things like, instead of being able to assign the best teachers to the students who need the most help, the best teachers say that they are already getting great results, they are not going to take a different class with weaker pupils. Whereas to a teacher who is really motivated, taking a class with weaker students is important.

I respect the observations you have made; I can totally believe what you say. But when people look at Singapore in terms of our overall average, I think you have to give credit to the fact that we are coming out with these amazing and astounding results in our education system. My only answer to this consultant in McKinsey was that it is because we have a system where we really try to motivate teachers and the principals with their mission of doing the best they can to develop the talents and abilities of the children under their charge. This is why, wherever you have new building sites under the MOE, you have this phrase on the hoardings: "Moulding the Future of Our Nation." I can assure you that this mission is drummed into teachers and principals all the time!

While I respect all the points that you are making, I am also saying that, as a whole, we ought to be quite proud of our success; what we need to do is to keep encouraging the teachers and the principals on the basis of, "Do the best that you can with the children in your charge. We know that you face difficulties; sometimes with MOE or with parents, but please do not be discouraged — we have to keep doing what is important for the children and their future. This is why you cannot be teaching the children just what is important for the exams at the end of the year, or what was important from the last ten years. Teachers must ask, 'What is important for the next 10 years? What is happening for the future, and what is the best way by which you can fit your children out for the future?'" That is what I have been trying to address in my lectures for Singapore and Singaporeans.

Now this other thing about saying, "How come people are chasing the money?" Well, you know, all of us would like to be doing jobs where we are paid at least reasonably and fairly for the job that we do. Indeed, it should always be the case that we are paid according to our performance, our contributions, what we do relative to what we are expected to do on the job. But the critical point I am making is that in every instance, we will only be paid according to that which our breadth of knowledge, experience, and skills today allows us to deliver in our performance. Chasing the money will only be about getting the most you can get for the skills, knowledge and experience you already have today.

But to progress and move up, we should always be looking out for opportunities to learn new things and opportunities to create new possibilities, because that is the way by which we become capable of accomplishing more. Chasing the opportunities opens new possibilities for the future; chasing the money limits us to what we are currently capable of.

GK: And in a nutshell, how did we lose that sense of public spiritedness or high-mindedness?

LSG: The quick answer in a nutshell is, "It was okay when I was there!" (laughter)

GK: Thank you, Mr Lim. You have been very generous with your time. You emphasised that it was the drive towards affluence that led to our progress. It was also the fixation with affluence that may cause our decline, and you have given us very many ideas as to how to ensure that we mitigate that decline, and tonight, how we can move to a new S-Curve, to a new Age of Pioneers.

So, Yoda, let me say this: The message, forcefully, you have spoken. Thinking and acting on the message, we will. The route to missed hope, we do not take. But certainly, follow the way of hope, we must, and we can, and it is believably achievable. Thank you, Sir!

About the Cover Illustrator

Caleb Tan ("Bucketcaleb") is an illustrator from Singapore. He graduated from the School of Technology for the Arts, Republic Polytechnic in 2009. Caleb illustrated a Singapore children's book with Direct Life Foundation and AF Storytellers, which was launched in 2016. He works closely with the Organisation of Illustrators Council (Singapore).